ESSAYS ON MUSIC

A.K. COOMARASWAMY

Essays on Music

Edited by
PREM LATA SHARMA

INDIRA GANDHI NATIONAL CENTRE FOR THE ARTS
NEW DELHI

MANOHAR
2010

First published 2010

ISBN 81-7304-611-5

Published by
Indira Gandhi National Centre for the Arts
Janpath, New Delhi 110001
in association with
Ajay Kumar Jain *for*
Manohar Publishers & Distributors
4753/23 Ansari Road, Daryaganj
New Delhi 110002

Typeset by
A J Software Publishing Co. Pvt. Ltd.
New Delhi 110005

Printed at
Lordson Publishers Pvt. Ltd.
Delhi 110007

Contents

Preface

I had been collecting Dr. A.K. Coomaraswamy's Writings on Indian music for several years, from sources in India, Sri Lanka and abroad. The manuscript containing his essays on music was entrusted to Prof. Prem Lata Sharma for editing and contributing an Introduction. Despite her indifferent health, she completed the task in 1998, and gave me the edited press copy of the present volume. But before she could see the labour of her work in print unfortunately she passed away the same year. It is now my painful duty to write a Preface for the work done by her. She had earlier meticulously edited another of Coomaraswamy's book entitled *Thirty Songs from the Panjab and Kashmir*, which was published in 1994.

The earliest records of Indian music are found in the *Ṛg Veda*. The drum, the flute, and the lute are mentioned. The chanting of the *Sāma Veda* shows that vocal music was considerably developed. The form of the Vedic chants is fixed, and constant throughout India. Indian music is a part of the national life, it is still an art. According to Coomaraswamy, 'Music is the most complete expression of the soul or genius of the Indians—a mirror faithfully reflecting their inner life'.

Coomaraswamy was among the lovers and admirers of Indian music who tried in the early days of the twentieth century, to present its character and basic structures to the English and later American audiences. His interest in Indian music was further strengthened by his second wife Alice Richardson, who accompanied him to India in 1911, and learnt Indian music from a traditional *ustad*. She used an Indian name, Ratan Devi. During the New York theatre season in 1916 onward, Ratan Devi was giving recitals of Indian music and dance in association with a Eurasian dancer, Roshanara.

In comparing the music of East and West, Coomaraswamy held that in harmony and combined effects, the West excels in a field which is almost unknown to the East, but on the other hand, there can be no doubt that in individual singing, whether technique, expression, or subtlety, the East far exceeds the West. Each has much to learn from, and admire in the other. W.B. Yeats has said that Indian music, though its theory is elaborate, and its technique so difficult, is not an art, but life itself.

New Delhi
August 2003

LALIT M. GUJRAL

Introduction

CRITICAL ANALYSIS OF CONTENTS

A.K. Coomaraswamy's perceptions on Indian music have a permanent value as well as a distinct historical setting on account of their expression having come at a time when a radical change in attitudes, modes of patronization and association with mechanization was visible. The period covered in these writings is from 1908-31. This period was marked by the following features that have been noticed by Coomaraswamy with great intensity:

1. Introduction of the gramophone in the last quarter of the nineteenth century and harmonium, the latter having come earlier.
2. Appreciation of and glamour for Western instruments like the piano and its music and despise for Indian music and its instruments, not only among the colonial rulers but also among 'educated' Indians.
3. Shift of the gravity of patronization from the aristocrat and the temple to the urban middle class which is cut off from its cultural roots.
4. Growth of the university system of education, borrowed from the British, which had no place for music.
5. A study of selected topics from *saṅgīta-śāstra* like *śruti.*
6. Widespread impact of mechanization in general which involves division of labour and deprives the worker from the joy of creating a whole piece.

Gramophone has now been far superseded by audio and video cassettes, compact discs, radio, television, etc. Amplification, preservation, reproduction and dissemination of sound is now possible in so many ways that the gramophone is almost out of date. The harmonium has come to stay with regained vigour after its re-introduction in All India Radio in the mid-seventies where it was banned after independence. All the same, it cannot be denied that the most perfect mechanization cannot replace the live voice of the human being or a musical instrument. The above gadgets have not improved, rather they have impaired our sensibility to the purity of sound. The lamenting of Coomaraswamy over the introduction of gramophone is more than a hundred-fold valid in the current situation.

Classical Western music is not widely known in India but contemporary jazz, pop and rap music are a craze among the younger generation. Movements like Spic-Macay are trying in their own way to inculcate an appreciation for Indian classical music and dance in schools and colleges but the glamour for 'modern' music is far too powerful.

His observations on the primary position occupied by oral tradition in the transmission of Indian music are equally valid today. No system of notation or mechanical device can replace it.

Patronization has shifted from the aristocracy and temples to the urban middle class. In the post-Independence era, government agencies like Departments of Culture, Sangeet Natak Akademis, Indian Council for Cultural Relations, etc., and business houses that have stepped in only recently represent the latest modes of patronization. The bureaucrat, the manager, the middle-man and the like are new faces of patrons. It is strongly felt by sensitive individuals interested in the preservation of the cultural heritage of India that the pursuit of music, dance and theatre cannot be left to the mercy of market forces. To quote the Haksar Committee report, 1990, p. 21,

> . . . this cultural production has been accomplished in a social context in which the mass media and the market have emerged as arbiters of taste and quality in aesthetic activity. Having separated art from the artisan, modern economies have converted art itself into a commodity, often mass-produced, like any other material goods. . . . In the generation of cultural values—more so than in the generation of material values—the market needs to be tamed and harnessed to serve the interest of man, nature and society.

All the above attempts of patronization have emerged to counter the market forces but they have entailed a new set of problems which need not be discussed here.

The number of universities in India started growing in the first quarter of the twentieth century and their number swelled after Independence. Music departments in universities were established from 1950 onwards and their number has been multiplying. By and large, their main thrust has borne the impact of non-statutory teaching and examining bodies which preceded them by two to three decades. They have brought about a lot of proliferation in respect of the number of music students but the objectives have not been clear and this proliferation cannot be said to have been conducive to the setting of standards.

The study of *saṅgīta-śāstra* in the first quarter of the twentieth century was solely centred around twenty-two *śrutis* and Coomaraswamy has duly noticed Shri Deval's work towards demonstration of *śrutis* through a specially constructed harmonium.

His sensitivity to the creative faculty of the human being was deeply hurt by the division of labour and drudgery that are in-built in the process of mechanization and in the process of production of various goods. The joy of creating a whole object is lost in this process and he has emphasized this point in his inimitable style.

VALUE OF THIS COMPILED REPRINT

The material compiled in this small volume is invaluable not only for providing a critical appraisal of the developments in the late nineteenth and early twentieth centuries affecting music in particular and culture in general, but also for the keen insights into the fundamentals of Indian culture that are profusely available. This volume will be of interest and profit not only to students of music but also to all those who are interested in Indian history and culture.

EDITORIAL POLICY

1. The essays have been arranged in four groups, viz., I. General Observations on Indian Music and Comments on the Contemporary Situation, II. Antiquity of *Viṇā* and its Description, III. Miscellaneous Writings, and IV. Appendices. Items like newspaper reports, letters, etc., have been included in Section A of the Appendix. Section B contains an article on 'Coomaraswamy's thoughts on Indian music' by K.C. Kamaliah. And, for A.K. Coomaraswamy's appreciation of traditional music three articles on 'Music in Ceylon', '*Thevaram* According to Pann' and '*Thevaram*' have also been included in this section.

   All the items have been put in a chronological order, group-wise.
2. Footnotes have been added for updating some points or by way of explanation.
3. Important lines have been placed in italics.
4. Repetition of passages, wherever located, have been indicated.

ACKNOWLEDGEMENTS

Dr. (Smt.) Kapila Vatsyayan, Academic Director, Indira Gandhi National Centre for the Arts, with her broad vision and deep understanding of Indian culture has planned a reprint series of the complete works of A.K. Coomaraswamy. The present volume forms part of this comprehensive scheme. I am grateful to her and to Dr. L.M. Gujral, Hony. Advisor, IGNCA, for giving me this opportunity of coming in contact with the great and versatile mind that was Coomaraswamy. I have thoroughly enjoyed reading his writings on Indian music for the corroboration that they have provided to my own humble thinking and for the guidance available therein for further thought.

My thanks are due to Dr. Niharika Lal for her assistance in editing this volume.

Amnaya, 209/1,
Karaundi, Varanasi 5
9 July 1998

PREM LATA SHARMA

I. GENERAL OBSERVATIONS ON INDIAN MUSIC AND COMMENTS ON THE CONTEMPORARY SITUATION

1. Indian Music*

> We have harmonies which you have not, of quarter-sounds, and lesser slides of sounds: divers instruments likewise to you unknown, some sweeter than any you have.
>
> BACON'S *New Atlantis*

Some time ago I contributed to the *Ceylon University Journal*, a 'Plea for the Teaching of Indian Music in Ceylon'. The appreciation of music has almost died out in Ceylon since the rule of the last Kandyan kings. The last king was fond of music, and like other Eastern rulers, kept a band of court musicians, singers, dancers, and players on instruments. But almost the only music now to be heard in Sinhalese Ceylon, beside the agricultural songs, is the daily *tevava* or musical service in viharas and devales (Buddhist temples and those of the Hindu gods worshipped by Buddhists in Ceylon). In this music three kinds of drums, cymbals, and oboes are used; these are also to be heard at festivals, and in processions. The music is good of its kind, especially the drumming; the general effect in procession is something like that of a drum and fife band, cheerful and inspiring. But as representing Indian music, it is quite inadequate; and good as the agricultural songs may be, they are very simple and slight; and singing is not studied by any other of the Sinhalese people at the present day.

Much the same is true of the Tamils in Ceylon. In Jaffna it is almost impossible to hear good music, other than the temple music of drums and oboes, and the singing of two or three skilled dancing girls. In Colombo it is not possible to hear the last, as dancing girls are no longer connected with the Hindu temples there. In Jaffna the *vīṇā* and *saraṅgī*, the best and sweetest of Indian instruments, are practically unknown. In some mission schools a little piano and singing of hymns is done; but the so-called Christian lyrics, which do represent some attempt to make use of Indian airs, are but the faintest echo of the real thing. Western music in English schools indeed, is regarded only as an elegant accomplishment in most cases, and is rarely anything more. There are girls whose parents have asked that they might learn 'a few strokes on the violin before they left!' just as they learn 'a little French' without ever expecting to speak to a Frenchman or read a French book. So that there was need indeed to plead (quite vainly, no doubt) with the people, and the Department of Public Instruction, for the teaching of Indian Music in Ceylon.

What of music in India herself? It is simply a question of whether or not Indian music can be saved before it is too late! The great danger of modern education in India is its ideal of purely material prosperity in the case of

* Reproduced from *Hindustan Review*, December 1908, pp. 248-60.

secular (Government) schools and colleges, and the refusal or inability to recognize any responsibility to the past in almost all missionary institutions. The consequent break in the continuity of the historical tradition is fatal to Indian culture. To take music as the special case: it is probable that there is not in India any educational institution under European inspiration, where Indian music has any place whatever in the scheme of education. There is no Indian university where the existence of Indian music, or its importance in Indian culture are recognized.[1] Of Europeans engaged in education in India, it is safe to say that less than 1 per cent (if so many) have any knowledge of it as a science, or any appreciation of it as an art. By most, it is quite frankly regarded as mere noise and clamour. It is only one illustration of the unfitness of Englishmen to control Indian education; they are unfitted alike by lack of knowledge and by lack of sympathy. The right place for English teachers in India now, whatever it may have been in the past, is in the employ of Indian educationalists. We should engage them for special purposes, as is done in Japan, and not allow them to control, where they do not understand or sympathize. It is of infinitely more importance for us to control the education of our children, than it is for us to control our own trade. It is better to be bare of wealth than to be bare of ideas. Swadeshi in the economic sphere moreover will assuredly follow swadeshi in education; for no small part of the national expenditure today goes to buy foreign-made articles which India does not really require, and from the possession of which she does not benefit, but very much the reverse. A generation of really national education would go further towards restoring the degraded taste which makes possible the purchase of quantities of the cheap and vulgar manufactures of Europe—clothing, furniture, cut glass, dyes, etc., and towards the re-establishment of the national handicrafts, than three generations of mere agitation and crying of 'Boycott', however useful and necessary these may be. In the case of music for example, if a healthy taste could be restored, through a re-vivification of the national culture, it would no longer be necessary for India to spend annually 13 lakhs of rupees on imported musical instruments, including pianos, violins, and, more especially, harmoniums and gramophones, the universal popularity of which last, is such damning evidence of the growing vulgarization of Indian taste. While small Indian capitalists are in a position to exploit the national sentiment by making wretched imitations of good English paper, nibs, or soap, the skilled craftsman, in this case the maker of musical instruments, is starving for want of occupation, and his hereditary knowledge, a definite asset in the national credit, is passing away for ever. While groups of well-meaning individuals are busy making bad Swadeshi biscuits, and others sacrifice a few pice per pound to buying them, the carver of wood, the ivory inlayer, the drawer of wire and the professional musician are all neglected for the travesties of music performed on harmoniums or lily flutes, or reproduced *ad nauseam* on gramophones, the profit on whose manufacture goes out of India. Do not suppose it would be any advantage to make them locally. The hope of reviving trade by reproducing locally any article that may come into fashion, without regard to its real value, is as delusive as it is mean.

It is never an advantage to a nation to produce useless or vicious luxuries; it does not increase the national wealth. By the time your harmonium factory is doing well, and Indians in it, working seventeen hours a day, are producing for the shareholders a dividend of 35 per cent (as in the Bombay cotton mills), some European or American invents a 'harmoniola' or something equally insane, cheaper and easier to play,—and where are you then? But no foreigner could make for you a *vīṇā*, or paint or inlay it with ivory, or carve for it a figure of Saraswatī; those are things which European or American factories cannot do.

Do not think that the desire for continual change is any evidence of progress. The eternal things are always with us. It is not Indian instruments which are to blame if we cannot express through them today, or recognize when heard the expression of the great emotions that the past uttered in no other way. As, in Europe, the violin cannot at any cost be better made today than it was made two hundred years ago, as too the violin will assuredly outlast the piano, so we may doubt if the *vīṇā* can ever be improved upon as a medium for the expression of emotion in terms of Indian music. The difficulty is other than that; it is that India does not any longer desire to express emotion in terms of art at all; India is content with mechanism, and a purely material ideal of prosperity.

Only the call of the Motherland will waken into music the silent lute and voice. The new music will not be played on the harmonium, or reproduced upon the gramophone. It will be played on Indian instruments, and be a live thing in the hearts of Indian men and women. *If* new instruments are needed to express new feelings, or to vary the manner of expression of old—and it is harder to think that Indians could outgrow the *vīṇā*, than to imagine that Europe could outgrow the violin—will not the people whose genius evolved the *vīṇā* itself, from whom indeed came the prototype of almost every European instrument, be able to respond? Or is the present death in life of Indian creative genius to last for ever, and are we never to do anything again but copy and copy? If that be so, let us at least copy something good, that we may keep alive the memory of beauty that was with us once. For Indian music, like Indian art and literature and philosophy, is one essential expression of Indian culture and civilization. By civilization we may broadly understand, the production of civil persons, in every true sense of the word. That the present neglect of Indian music does not illustrate the progress of such civilization, is within the experience of all of us. A Tamil lady sang for me once some Sanskrit and Tamil hymns. But her son, who attended the Government college, where such things as his own music and his own language were not taught or mentioned, had neither the wish to listen, nor the respect which should have kept him silent; he worked a gramophone all the time his mother sang. How utterly impossible such a situation would once have been! One is led to wonder sometimes whether it is civilization or barbarism that the West is bringing to the East.

It would be impossible to explain to one not already familiar with Indian life, in what countless ways music has been bound up with the national culture. It is the most universal expression of emotion, religious, amorous or martial.

Music belonged to every part of life. The flute of Krishna, the *vīṇā* of Saraswati; the dance of Siva; the Gayatri as cosmic chant or music of the spheres; the hymns of passionate adoration of the Southern Saivite, all these belong to the association of music and religion. Song and agriculture, too, are intimately connected; in Ceylon, for example, as you walk along some narrow village track, you may come suddenly upon a hillside clearing where twenty or thirty men are working, and singing at their work, led by an old man with a quavering voice; or a row of stooping women weeding, and singing as they progress steadily across the field in the hot sun; at work in a wet field transplanting rice. Such scenes did not escape the notice of Sinhalese poets; a mediaeval version of the Makha Deva Jataka relates that as a certain prince went on his way, he saw 'hundreds of girls tending the ear-laden fields, singing sweet songs without fault, wherein his own life was praised'. One such song relates the exploits of a national hero named Gaja Bahu; in another well-known song, the tala palm is praised.

> In Rayigam Korale renowned there grew a famous tala-palm,
> Fairer than speech can tell.
>
> With various beauty crowned,
> From village unto village known;
>
> Fair of hue this palm-flower bloomed.
> As it were lotus petals expanded on the tree.

The half religious character of many of the agricultural songs is very noteworthy; one sowing song begins as follows—'When the fields are well prepared, which lie round Balagala hill, right quickly then the seed is sown by Four Regents of the Earth'. A threshing song runs 'This is not our threshing floor, 'tis the Moon-god's threshing floor; this is not our threshing floor, 'tis the Sun-god's threshing floor.' Such songs are the fruit of that 'pagan' conception of all life as a sacrament, which gives in the East so much beauty and dignity to common things. What more perfect picture can one have of the simple agricultural life of an Indian village, than the bright-moonlight threshing floor, freshly cleaned and consecrated, where the corn is trodden out by the feet of bulls driven round a 'bull-post' in the middle? Even the bulls are in the song—

> O bull-king, leader of the team,
> O Veriya going next him.
> And Kalata the bull-calf,
> Make haste to get the threshing done
> I will get your twin horns gilt,
> Deck your pair of ears with pearls,
> And eke your dew-claws,

So shall I adorn ye!
Ye bulls that wander by the hillside,
Yoked together by a woodbine,
Wearing pearls and coral beads,
And eating tender leaves, . . .
Draw the grain into this threshing floor!

Such are the agricultural songs. Simple as they are, those who have heard them in their own surroundings, will not easily forget them. But even these are less used than formerly, and in time will be gone.

There is this character in Indian music, that it speaks directly to the feelings.

For all their musike bothe that they play upon instrumentes, and that they singe with mannes voyce dothe so resemble and expresse natural affections, the sound of the tune is so applied and made agreable to the things, that whether it bee a prayer, or els a dytty of gladnes, of patience, of trouble, of mourninge, or of anger: the fassion of the melodye dothe so represente the meaning of the thing, that it doth wonderfullye move, stirre, pearce, and enflame the hearers myndes. (More's Utopia)

Music indeed has been thought to have power even over animals and inanimate things. Stories of the influence of certain *rāgas* over nature recall the legends of Orpheus and Apollo.[2] How profound and intimate has been the appeal of Eastern music to the East, may be guessed from such stories, and the many other references in oriental literature.

The tenderness of all Eastern music is suggested in a wonderful passage from the Arabian Nights. The Cairene singer in the tale of Miriam and Ali Nur-ud-din had an Indian lute kept in a satin bag with slings of gold; she opened and shook it,

whereupon there fell thereout two and thirty pieces of wood, which she fitted one into another, male into female and female into male, till they became a polished lute of Indian workmanship. Then she uncovered her wrists and laying the lute in her lap, bent over it with the bending of mother over babe, and swept the strings with her fingertips; whereupon it moaned and resounded and after its olden home yearned; and it remembered the waters that gave it drink and the earth whence it sprang and wherein it grew, and it minded the carpenters who cut it and the polishers who polished it, and the merchants who made it their merchandise and the ships that shipped it; and it cried and called aloud and moaned and groaned; and it was as if she asked it of all these things and it answered her with the tongue of the case.

Indian music can best be heard, and dancing seen, in the great Southern cities such as Madura and Tanjore, and in the native states, Mysore and Travancore. In such places it is still studied as a science by learned Brahmans and patronized by princes. You may engage a dancing girl and her musicians, and invite your friends; seated upon a carpet in a room bare of all useless furniture, your entertainment is more wonderful than any that money could buy in any other land; more wonderful at least for you, for it is one expression of that national culture of which you too are a part; it is your love and your emotion, your adoration for the Lord which the dancer dances and the singer sings. Another time she is to sing only for you; she brings a *tamburi* or a *vīṇā*, and seated like you upon the ground, pours out for as long as you will without fatigue, songs of passionate love; or devotion moving you to tears.

Suppose that it is a man who plays or sings for you; one who has wandered from court to court and received the rewards of princes and kings. He plays the *sāraṅgī* as none else can; the Kashmir shawl he wears is the token of a raja's favour. There are no young men following in his steps; it is well to hear him while you may. In the north he will be perhaps a player on the *taus*, the 'peacock'. He too sings a song of passionate love, something at once so simple and so universal that it includes the love of God and the love of woman; it is part of the method of Indian poetry to carry double meanings, of which each deepens and explains the other, like the shot colours of a double woven cloth. There are only four of you listening, and to-night you think only of devotion to the Lord, for that thought is in the singer's heart, and he is carried away by his own emotion and neither sees nor thinks of you. And if one in his heart thinks only of his beloved on earth yet for him too is each love the symbol and revelation of the other.

> I am mad for my beloved: they say, what say they? Let them say what they will!
> Take me for a fool or a mad man; they say, what say they? Let them say what they will!
> I have nothing to do with them,
> Whether they be pleased with me or angry,
> May one only be gracious to me!
> They say, what say they? Let them say what they will!
> The Shaikh walks around his sanctuary;
> I offer up myself at thy altar,
> Call it sanctuary or den.
> They say, what say they? Let them say what they will!
> I have gazed on the glory and sheen of the cheeks of my beloved,
> I am burnt up as a moth in the flame,
> I am as one drunken:
> They say, what say they? Let them say what they will!

So simple is the cry; but it tells alike of the love of those great ones who 'are so enchanted with the beauty of the Creator of appearances, that they have nothing to do with the beauty of appearance itself', and of those with whom all the kingdoms of the earth weigh less than a feather in the scale against one woman only, upon whom their heart is set. It is for every sect and every man.

Even this is not the most wonderful experience which Indian music holds for those that have ears to hear. There is a music which comes once or twice only to you, and which it is vain to seek. The very greatest of Indian musicians are not professionals, but wandering holy men, players of the *taus* or *sāraṅgī* or *vīṇā*, or singers. Some evening in a northern town such a one passes by your door. You press him eagerly to lodge with you, if he will, to play for you, and he consents. You invite a few friends, and seated on the floor in an upper room, prepare to listen. A brass lamp burns by your side, and all is still. The player chooses an even simpler theme than the last,—'These many days I have not seen thee.' He sings and plays, and varies infinitely the expression of this one idea. He becomes a part of this instrument, and it and the sound of him. You lose consciousness of things external, and forget to move the wick, which burns dimly and more dimly still. As he plays on—'These many days I have not seen thee', this passionate cry materializes before your eyes as a dancing figure, it may be as the Lord Krishna Himself, it may be as Radha, it may be in the form of one beloved on earth, whomsoever your thoughts are set upon, and to whom your love is given. You forget all else, and seen only this rhythmic sweet appearance. At last the player ceases, leaving you silent and breathless, and the vision is gone like a dream. What did you see? You ask of one another, and you find that each saw before him his own thought, the one he loved best, and for whom in his heart was lamentation made,—'These many days I have not seen thee.'

Or it may be in the South. You have gone to a musical party, a wedding at the house of a friend, you are seated with many others on the cotton carpet, and before you is a band of drummers, oboists and players of the *vīṇā* and *tamburi*. A handsome Brahman drums on an earthen pot. A slender girl of fifteen years sits demurely on the floor, dressed in silk brocade and golden chains, her feet and arms bare, and flowers in her hair. Her mother is seated near, back against the wall; she it is that trained the girl, and now she watches her proudly. The only sounds are those of the four strings of the ivory inlaid *tamburi* and the tapping of a drum. As you are waiting for the music to begin, a man with untidy hair and a saffron robe comes in, and your host gives him eager welcome, laying a white cloth on a stool for him to sit upon. All know him well—he is a sannyasi who wanders from temple to temple, preaching little, nor performing many ceremonies, but singing tevaram and the hymns of Manikka Vasagar. As he sits silent, all eyes are turned towards him, and conversation drops to a whisper. Presently he sings some hymn of passionate adoration of Siva. His voice is thin but very sweet, melting the heart; his gentle strong personality holds every listener spellbound, not least the little dancer to whom the words and music are so familiar; he is the dancer's and the drummers' friend and hero as much as yours. Someone asks for a special hymn, 'My God, why hast thou forsaken me?' and he sings.

> Me, meanest one, in mercy mingling Thou didst make Thine own,
> Lord of the Bull! Lo, Thou'st forsaken me! O Thou who wear'st
> Garb of fierce tiger's skin! Abiding Uttarakoca-mangai's King!
> Thou of the braided lock! I fainting sink. Our Lord, uphold thou me!
> What though I press no more the crimson lips of maidens fair,
> With swelling breasts; behold! Thou hast forsaken me; though in,
> Not out Thy worthy service, Uttara-koca-mangai's King,
> I am! Thou mad'st false me Thine own, why dost Thou leave me now?[3]

Soon he rises, smiles at the musicians and speaks for a few moments with your host, and so goes away. And then you forget for a time this dreamer, in the beauty of the dance and the clamour of the drums. Of the dance you never weary; there is eternal wonder in the perfect refinement of its grace, and the mental concentration needed to control each muscle so completely; for this is not the passionate posturing born of a passing mood, but the elaborated art of three thousand years, an art that deceives you by its seeming simplicity, but in reality idealizes every passion, human and divine; for it tells of the intensity of Radha's love for Krishna, Radha was leader of the herd-girls in Brindaban, and she, more than any, realized the depth and sweetness of the love of Krishna.

Hers was the frank and instant recognition, the deep understanding, and the constant vision of His glory. And she it was who reached the unutterable depths of sorrow, when the simple joys of that peasant-world could hold Him no longer, and He left Brindaban for ever, to return to the life and responsibility of kings, freeing His people from the tyrant of Mathura. Wherefore, because of this wondrous union between the human soul of Radha and the Divine in Krishna, all love has come to be summed up in Their love. And when the Infinite whispers Its secrets to the finite—as happens to all of us sometimes in loving—the moment is expressed in Indian poetry, as the speech of Krishna the Cowherd with Radha, leader of the Gopis.

And so both have told of the Lord,—the ascetic, for whom all earthly beauty is a vain thing, and the dancing girl, who is mistress of every art that charms the senses.

The music is to last all night; but you have to be home ere dawn, and as you pass along the road in the bright moonlight, you see that life, and the renunciation of life, lead both to the same goal at last. Both ascetic and musician shall be one Brahman with Himself; it is only a question of time, more, or less, and time, as every one knows, is unreal.

On Lord, look not upon my evil qualities!
Thy name, O Lord, is same-sightedness,
Make us both one Brahman.

This Hindi song of Sūrdās is said to have been sung by a dancing girl at a Rajput court. And there comes to you too the thought, that 'Whoso seeth all beings in That One, and That in all, shall no more shrink from any.' All this is passing away; when it is gone, men will look back on it with hungry eyes, as some have looked upon the life even of mediaeval Europe, or of Greece. When civilization has made of life a business, it will be remembered that life was once an art; when culture is the privilege of bookworms it will be remembered that it was once a part of life itself, not something achieved in stolen moments of relief from the serious business of being an engine-driver, a clerk, or a Governor. 'The old culture came to a man at his work; it was not at the expense of life, but an exaltation of life itself.' Let those who are still part of such a life take note of it, that they may tell their children of it when it is nothing but a memory. A 'practical' and 'respectable' world has no place for the dreamer and the dancer; they belong to the old quiet Hindu towns where the big temples and the *chatrams* tell of the faith and munificence of kings and merchant princes. In Madras there is the military band, or the music hall company on tour, what does it want with ascetics or with dancing girls?

A serious blow was given to Indian music in the north, by the puritanism and intolerance of certain of the Mughal rulers. One day the minstrels of

Delhi paraded through the streets with a bier. Asked by Aurangzeb what they meant, they said that Music was dead, and must be buried; 'Bury him deep,' replied the Emperor, 'that no sound may ever rise from him.' Calvinism has not been confined to Scotland! But Akbar was wiser, and is said not only to have patronized Hindu musicians, but to have been a maker of music himself. Shah Jahan, too, gave to a certain minstrel his weight in gold as fee for his great playing.

A heavier blow has been struck than Aurangzeb's. Indian music, like the other expressions of Indian culture has gone down, for a time or for ever, before the material ideals of Western Civilization. Successful mechanism has so hypnotized the East that it is blind to its own slavery.[4] So too in the West, but the West may save itself at last; it cannot save India. India must save itself.

Music has been always the delight of Hindu kings. At their courts were to be found the best musicians. Whatever the luxury or corruption of some Indian courts may have been, they were centres of culture. The place of the royal craftsmen, pandits, astronomers and musicians was assured; their maintenance belonged to the ideal of kingly state. Culture was thus state-endowed, and pursued its way undisturbed by political events. When the Indian courts were done away with, and Indian rulers succeeded by British Governors, all this intellectual and artistic life was undermined. The English Governor with his efficiency and his reforms, needed no minstrels and no craftsmen; all that he needed was a supply of clerks. Compare the state of Tanjore today with the evidence of the rule of the Hindu Rajas; the great library neglected, a dead thing not being added to or playing a great part in the growth of national culture; the royal musicians dispersed, and the famous collection of splendidly decorated and ancient musical instruments also dispersed; the fine weaving done for the court a thing of the past; the training and the emoluments of administrative office in the hands of foreigners to whom the old life and the old culture mean little or nothing, it is a strange evidence of the greatness of Western Civilization and the grandeur of British rule in India, that it should so often appear as the destroyer of culture! Even in Native States the same process is going on; false ideals of economy or efficiency, still more false taste have led to the dispersal of the musicians and neglect of Indian music; what does a Maharajah want with the common music that any one can hear, when he can spend hundreds of pounds on gorgeous gramophones? The Raja of today, with his French palaces and his tutor, the Resident, has too often most of the vices, more than the weakness, and little of the dignity of his predecessors. What great work Indian princes might yet do for the Indian people, in preserving the national culture; but they first of all have hurried to dispense with it. Well the king-days are over; it is vain to put your trust in princes; the national culture must be preserved by the people if it is to be preserved at all. But at present, the lives of the so-called educated, the professional classes in India, are extraordinarily material in their aims, and narrow in their outlook. India, 'progressive India', does not want art; she wants desperately to be practical.

NOTES

1. Since 1950, departments of music in Indian universities have been gradually established, Banaras and Baroda being the pioneers. Gradually, the number of these departments has been swelling.—Ed.
2. Some of these are quoted by C.R. Day, in his *Music and Musical Instruments of Southern India and the Deccan*, 1891.
3. Translation by Dr. Pope, but made more literal in the second verse.
4. As in the story of the Chinese Emperor, for whom was made a magnificent mechanical nightingale. Its song was pronounced finer by far than that of the living bird. But by degrees the mechanism wore out, and at last failed altogether; and when the Emperor lay dying, deserted by his favourites, none came to comfort him but the despised living bird!

2. Indian Music*

> We have harmonies which you have not, of quarter sounds, and lesser slides of sounds: divers instruments likewise to you unknown, some sweeter than any you have.
>
> BACON'S *New Atlantis*

> The introduction of a new kind of music must be shunned as imperilling the whole state; since styles of music are never disturbed without affecting the most important political institutions.
>
> PLATO, *Republic*

The earliest records of Indian music are found in the *Rig Veda.* The drum, the flute and the lute are mentioned. Instrumental music was performed at certain religious rites; the lute (*vīṇā*) was played at the sacrifice to the *manes.* The existence of several kinds of professional musicians is implied in the *Yajur Veda.* The chanting of the *Sama Veda* shows that vocal music was considerably developed.

In later times, references to music in the Sanskrit and Pāli books abound. In the sculptures of Amarāvatī and Sāñcī and the paintings of Ajantā are represented instruments almost identical with those in use at the present day. There are also represented one or two instruments of an Assyrian or Egyptian type, particularly a kind of harp, not now in use.

The prototypes of most or all European instruments in use at the present day are still to be found in the East, the source of the foundations of so much of western culture. The Greeks attributed the greater part of their science of music to India.[1] Notwithstanding the differences between modern and ancient Hindu music, it is probable that the music of Southern India is more akin to ancient Greek music than any other music remaining in the world.[2] Not only is this the case in respect of structure and theory, but as regards the point of view from which music is regarded. Of the Greeks it has been said, that

> inferior to the moderns in the mechanical resources of the art, they had made, it appears, a far finer and closer analysis of its relation to emotional states; with the result that even in music, which we describe as the purest of the arts, congratulating ourselves on its absolute dissociation from all definite intellectual conceptions, the standard of the Greeks was as much ethical as Aesthetic, and the style of music was distinguished and its value appraised, not only by the pleasure to be derived from it, but also by the effect it tended to produce on character.

Of this attitude Mr. Dickinson remarks 'that moral effects should be attributed to music and to dancing, and that these should be regarded as of

* A.K. Coomaraswamy, *Essays in National Idealism,* Colombo, 1909.

such importance as to influence profoundly the whole constitution of a state, will appear to the majority of modern men an unintelligible paradox'.[3] An acquaintance with Indian music would make such conceptions less incomprehensible. The fine and close analysis of the relation of music to emotional states is particularly characteristic; and when we realize the part that music plays in Indian life, how far more inseparably it is bound up with poetry than is the case in the modern West; how it enters equally into the daily life of king and peasant, how it is felt to be the natural expression of all deep emotion and finally how, as explained below, the neglect or decay of Indian music is, as in the case of other arts, inseparably associated with a loss of stability in the economic structure of society, we may believe that Plato spoke advisedly in saying that styles of music are never disturbed without affecting the most important political institutions.

A suggestion made by Lafcadio Hearn respecting Japan, holds good also for India; reading 'Indian' for 'Japanese', I quote: 'to witness the revival of some perished Greek civilisation . . . were not any more of a privilege than is the opportunity actually afforded to us to-day to study Indian life'. I often think it strange that anthropologists and scientists so eagerly investigate the lives and culture of savage peoples, and neglect the great expressions of the human spirit, still remaining in the Eastern civilizations whose character is being changed so rapidly before our eyes. *It is, I suppose, a result of the European conviction that while it may be of interest to study others, it were absurd to think that anything could be learnt from them. Europe, indeed, cannot expect to learn much from India so long as she is convinced that her only mission is to teach.*

The golden age of Indian music, as of art, belongs to the early middle ages, perhaps from the fifth to the twelfth centuries. But in the South, owing to its comparative freedom from the influence of Persian music and from the puritanism of Islam, the science of music was cultivated more nearly in its original forms to a much later time, in some degree even to the present day.

Two causes have adversely affected Indian music in the later middle ages. One of these is the puritanism and intolerance of Islam, by which a serious injury was done to Indian music in the North. One day the minstrels of Delhi paraded through the streets with a bier. Asked by Aurangzeb what they meant, they said that Music was dead, and must be buried. 'Bury him deep,' replied this Calvin of Islam, 'that no sound may ever rise from him.'[4] But Akbar and Shah Jehan were men of broader culture; the former was himself a musician and composer, the latter is said to have rewarded a famous minstrel with a fee of his weight in gold.

Another cause of the neglect of Indian music has been its association with dancing girls and musicians of low-caste. This in many parts of India has led to an idea that music, like dancing, was not a becoming occupation for other persons, and there has resulted a neglect of its study in the homes of respectable families. Amongst dancing girls however, and by the musicians associated with them, both arts have been maintained in great perfection. A recent puritanical movement known as the 'Anti-nautch' movement has had a reverse influence.

In modern times, more injury has been done to Indian music by the stupidity of educationists, the snobbery of anglicized Indians, and the mechanism of commercial civilization, than could have been effected by many Aurangzebs. As we have seen, music has been always the delight of Hindu kings.[5] At their courts were to be found the best musicians. Whatever the luxury or corruption of some Indian courts may at times have been, they were always centres of culture. The place of the royal craftsmen, pandits, astronomers and musicians was assured; their maintenance belonged to the ideal of kingly state. Culture was thus state-endowed, and pursued its way undisturbed by political events. When the Indian courts were done away with, and Indian rulers succeeded by British Governors, all this intellectual and artistic life was undermined.[6] The English Governor with his efficiency and his reforms, needed no minstrels and no craftsmen; all that he needed was a supply of clerks. Compare the state of Tanjore today with the evidences of the rule of the Hindu Rajas; the great library neglected, a dead thing not being added to or playing a great part in the growth of national culture; the royal musicians dispersed, and the famous collection of splendidly decorated and ancient musical instruments also scattered; the fine weaving done for the court now forgotten; the training and the emoluments of administrative office in the hands of foreigners to whom the old life and the old culture mean little or nothing—it is a strange evidence of the greatness of Western Civilization and the grandeur of British rule in India, that it should so often appear as the destroyer of culture!

Even in Native States the same process is going on; false ideals of economy or efficiency, and a still falser taste have led to the dispersal of the musicians and neglect of Indian music; what does a Maharajah want with the common music that any one can hear, when he can spend hundreds of pounds on gorgeous gramophones and mechanical violins? The Raja of today, with his French palaces and his tutor, the Resident, has too often most of the vices, more than the weakness, and little of the dignity of his predecessors. Indian princes might yet do great work for the Indian people, in preserving the national culture; but they have hurried to dispense with it. The king-days are over; it is vain to put ones trust in princes; the national culture must be preserved by the people if it is to be preserved at all. But at present, the lives of the so-called educated, the professional classes in India, are extraordinarily material in their aims, and narrow in their outlook. India, 'progressive India', does not want art; she wants desperately to be practical.[7] Time will show whether she alone, and for the first time in history, can be or become great with such ideals.

Early Indian music, as explained in the Sanskrit books, appears to have differed much from the modern practice. Its principal feature was a division of the scale into 22 parts called *śruti,* of which four corresponded to a major tone, three to a minor, and two to a semitone. The modern theory, modes and notation are derived from the ancient; but 'the whole system has undergone a complete change and gradual refinement, until between the ancient and modern music there exists a difference as clearly marked and perceivable, to even the most casual observer, as that between the modern Anglican chant and the ancient Gregorian tones'.[8]

But there is music still in India. It is not too late to understand this intimate expression of Indian culture. The principal characteristics of modern Indian music are briefly as follows. The octave is divided into 12 semitones, as nearly as possible identical with the notes of European instruments, tuned to equal temperament.[9] From these twelve semitones, 72 scales or modes (*melakartās*) are formed; of these only 36 are in general use. A *rāga* or melody-type, is a 'melodic extension of certain notes of a particular scale or mode, according to certain fixed rules'; the number of *rāgas* is exceedingly large. Each is deemed to correspond to or awaken a particular definite emotion. Almost the only harmony consists in the use of a drone, a continuation of the low or dominant music as in the Scottish bagpipes. The seven notes of the Indian scale are named, in tonic sol-fa wise, *sa, ri, ga, ma, pa, dha, ni.* All that can be written down in this notation is the mere skeleton, or succession of notes proper to the *rāga.* Thus the text of the *rāga* 'Śrī' runs:

> Ascending mode: sa, ri, ma, pa, ni, sa.
> Descending mode: sa, ni, pa, dha, ni, pa, ma, ri, ga, ri, sa.

It will be seen that neither the relative values of the notes, accentuation, tempo, grace notes, or any other details can be thus indicated. These, composing what is called the *mūrcchanā* of the *rāga,* can be learnt only by hearing it actually performed, and are in fact so learnt, mainly through the medium of songs in the same *rāga.* There is thus in music that necessary dependence of the disciple upon the master, which is characteristic of every kind of education in India.

I have stated that the 12 semitones of modern Indian music are almost or quite the same as the 12 semitones of Western instruments. But it is said by others that the scale thus employed is a just scale and not the scale of equal temperament necessitated by the use of harmony:[10] and also that the notes based on a division of the octave into 22 *śrutis* are still employed,[11] and of this there can be little doubt. It is at least certain that attempts to write down Indian music in staff notation are generally failures.[12] This may be partly due to the survival of the use of quarter and third tones in the essential part of the melody. It is certainly partly due to the fact that the grace notes which play so important a part in Indian music are actually of this character.

A great part of the effect of Indian vocal music depends on the peculiar manner and the skill with which the singer dwells on certain notes, which are varied or trilled,—'vibrating like a bird above the water before it pounces upon its prey'—but not to the extent of a semitone above or below the main note. The same effect (*gamakam*) is produced in stringed instruments by varying the tension of the string by deflection.

Such effects, so intimately dependent, in the degree and manner of their expression, upon the musician's individual mood and powers, cannot be written down, and so it is that an Indian air, set down upon the staff and picked out note by note on a piano or harmonium[13] becomes the most thin and jejune sort of music that can be imagined, and many have abandoned in despair all such attempts at record. The music is moreover so personal, and so capable of variation according to the singer's mood, that no record can quite adequately interpret it. The same singer may vary his own rendering from verse to verse, and improvize upon the main theme according to his mood or environment.[14] It must therefore be understood that the examples given are merely suggestive illustrations, and do not make possible an accurate reproduction of the originals. The only way to adequately study Indian music, is at first hand, by patient discipleship, a practical acquaintance with the instruments, and the help of learned Indians.

All attempts at 'harmonizing' Indian airs, have been, so far, unsuccessful. Whatever the reasons, it has been proved by repeated experience that the natural beauties and national character of the melodies are lost in the process, and the result is something devoid of all the peculiar charm of the original, and lacking in the essential qualities of either Indian or European music. Even the employment of the piano or harmonium prove fatal to the delicacy and purity of Indian music, because of the limitation to exact and mechanically limited ranges of notes; and the harmonium especially from its destructive effect upon the quality of the voice and fatal effects on individual taste and refinement.

It is quite likely however, that when sufficient study is given to the matter, harmonization of Eastern music may be possible. On this point M. Bourgault-Ducondray in his *Melodies Populaires de Grèce* writes:

> We trust that we have been able to show that the application of harmony to Oriental scales is productive of result. Eastern music, till now exclusively melodic, will start upon a new harmonic career; Western harmonic music, hitherto restricted to the exclusive use of two modes, the major and minor, will escape at last from its long confinement. The fruit of this deliverance will be to provide Western musicians with fresh resources of expression, and with colours hitherto unknown to the palate of the musician.

Harmonization, if possible, with due regard to the preservation of the mode, will similarly add to the resources of the Indian musi ian.[15]

The impression conveyed by Indian music is that of a limpid purity of colour effect, and, compared with Western concerted music, suggests a comparison of refined and delicate Indian dyes with the brilliant variety of modern chemical colouring matters, or the flow of a deep river with the rush of a noisy torrent. Western music, apart from emphasis laid upon technique often at the expense of feeling, is complex, troubled, reflecting as it were many sides of life and thought at once. In Indian music the emotions are unmixed, and each in turn exerts its power. Of this sort must have been the music dreamt of by More in his *Utopia*, which in this respect might have been written of India.

For all their musike bothe that they play upon instrumentes, and that they singe with mannes voyce dothe so resemble and expresse natural affections, the sound of the tune is so applied and made agreable to the things, that whether it bee a prayer, or els a dytty of gladnes, of patience, of trouble, of mourninge, or of anger; the fassion of the melodye dothe so represente the meaning of the thing, that it doth wonderfullye move, stirre, pearce, and enflame the hearers myndes.

MORE'S *Utopia*

A little of the tenderness of Indian music is reflected in a passage from the Arabian Nights already quoted (p. 16).* Those who once fall beneath its sway are forever spellbound by its magic. For the modern world it is too perfect and too refined. It is more the misfortune than the fault of Europeans and Europeanized Indians that they cannot appreciate its beauty. Accustomed to the noisy music of an orchestra, the artificial atmosphere of an upholstered and crowded concert hall, and the complexity and variety of emotion awakened by the elaborate developments of modern Western music, it is not surprising that the delicacy and subjectivity of Indian music leave them little moved, or give only an impression of monotony.

If in comparing the music of East and West, it may be said that in harmony and combined effects the West excels in a field which is almost unknown to the East, there can on the other hand be no doubt that in individual singing, whether technique, expression or subtlety, the East far exceeds the West. Each has much to learn from, and to admire in, the other.

The Indian singer, as Miss MacCarthy (loc. cit.) says,

seems to concentrate upon his very inmost self in the exercise of his art. His eyes close often in prayerful ecstasy. His pauses are long and frequent. Those who accompany him hang upon his mood and follow its winding without any other support than that of intention. The audience too, must follow as best it can—*he* leads *it*, it does not lead him.

Much of this description is realized in an Indian painting (in the collection of the Raja of Satārā), representing the poet Sadi listening to a singer.

Whatever may be gained by possible combination in the future developments of Indian music, the necessity for this intensely personal and rhapsodical singing—so perfect and so natural an expression of the Indian mind—cannot pass away. It were well indeed if room could be found in the West, which, with all its magnificent choral and orchestral development, lacks this lyrical and intensely personal and religious element, for individual expressions of the same kind. To some extent, no doubt, the revival of folk song in England is due to a sense of this need at the present time.

It would be difficult to explain to a foreigner the countless ways in which music in India is bound up with the national culture. It is the resource of India in joy or sorrow. It is a symbol of the immanence of God. 'Thou art present even as music in the *vīṇā*' says a Tamil poet. It is essential at every festivity, and inseparably connected with all religious ceremonies. 'The Vedic chant, composed in the simple Sanskrit spoken three thousand years ago

* Ref. A.K. Coomaraswamy, *Essays in National Idealism*, p. 16.

and handed down from generation to generation for more than thirty centuries,... is to Hindus what plain song is to us. For this ancient chant, like plain song, is bound up with the sacred ceremonials and is wedded to language alike sonorous and dignified. And the place where it is heard, for it is heard only in the temple, is considered so holy, and the strain itself is so simple and devotional, that all who hear it cannot fail to be impressed.' The form of the Vedic chants is fixed, and constant throughout India, but this is not the case with other hymns such as those of the Southern Saivites, which are sung to many airs in the homes and temples of the south. Mānikka Vācagar's hymns are familiar to all and are sung with tears of rapture; there is a saying that 'he whose heart is not melted by the Tiruvāçagam must have a stone for a heart'.

Of dramatic music there is no lack. Certain classical dramas, Rāma Charitam, Arichandra [Harishchandra], and the like, are known to the whole people, lettered or illiterate, and appeal equally to both. The south Indian drama is of much importance in the life of the people; just as miracle and mystery plays in the life of Mediaeval Europe. But these representations are now often degraded by the use of cheap harmoniums, called in the south 'Lily-flutes', and by the use of unsuitable and tawdry European scenery and costume, imitations of those tenth-rate travelling companies.

Of special interest are the songs of agriculture and the crafts. By these, I mean all music serving to lighten heavy labour, such as the songs of husbandmen, carters and boatmen; songs embodying technical recipes, and serving as craft mnemonics; songs of invocation of craft or agricultural divinities, or expressing a sacramental conception of a craft; and religious songs,—such as used to be sung at 'spinning bees' in Ceylon before the village weaver's market was 'successfully contested' by the products of the wage-slaves of English factory towns. In all these songs music and words are inseparable. The greater part of Eastern literature, popular or otherwise, is written in verse, and verse implies song. Men and women may be illiterate; but when they can recite classical poetry for hours—in language differing at least as much, and in the same way from that in everyday use, as does the language of the Psalms or of Chaucer from the daily speech of an Englishman—then we can hardly deny them 'education'.

Song and agriculture are intimately associated; 'as you walk along some narrow village track, you may come suddenly upon a hillside clearing where twenty or thirty men are working, and singing at their work, led by an old man with a quavering voice; or a row of stooping women weeding, and singing as they progress steadily across the field in the hot sun, at work in a wet field transplanting rice. Such scenes did not escape the notice of Sinhalese poets; a mediaeval version of the Makhā Deva Jātaka relates that as a certain prince went on his way, he saw 'hundreds of girls tending the ear-laden fields, singing sweet songs without fault, wherein his own life was praised'. One song relates the exploits of a national hero named Gaja Bāhu. In a well-known reaping song, the *tala* palm is praised.

In Rayigam Korale renowned there grew a famous *tala*-palm,
  Fairer than speech can tell.

With various beauty crowned,
  From village unto village known;

Fair of hue this palm-flower bloomed,
  Like lotus petals blowing on the tree.

The religious character of many of the agricultural songs is very noteworthy; one sowing song begins as follows—'When the fields are well prepared, which lie round Balagala-hill, right quickly then the seed is sown by Four Regents of the Earth.' A threshing song runs: 'This is not our threshing floor, 'tis the Moon-god's threshing floor; this is not our threshing floor, 'tis the Sun-god's threshing floor.' Such songs are the fruit of that 'pagan' conception of all life as a sacrament, which gives in the East so much beauty and dignity to common things. What more perfect picture can be imagined of the simple agricultural life of an Indian village, than the bright moonlit threshing-floor, freshly cleaned and consecrated, where the corn is trodden out by the feet of bulls driven round a 'bull-post' in the middle? Even the bulls are in the song.

O bull-king, leader of the team,
  O Veriya going next him,
And Kalata the bull-calf,
  Make haste to get the threshing done!
I will get your twin horns gilt,
  Deck you pair of ears with pearls,
And eke your dew-claws,
  So shall I adorn ye!
Ye bulls that wander by the hillside,
  Yoked together by a woodbine,
Wearing pearls and coral beads,
  And eating tender leaves, . . .
Draw the grain into this threshing floor!

'Such are the agricultural songs. Simple as they are, those who have heard them in their own surroundings, will not easily forget them. But even these are less used than formerly, and in a little time will be gone.'[16]

Women transplanting rice in the wet fields of Ceylon, sing *jātakas*, and other songs about the Buddha; *Samanala hella* (the song of Adam's Peak); *Padmāvatī kathāva*—the loveliest of Sinhalese princesses who became a Rajput bride and *sati*; others, sung by Kandyan women transplanting rice, include a number of *jātakas*.

Music has been thought to have power even over animals and inanimate things. How profound and intimate has been the appeal of Eastern Music to the East, may be guessed from stories of the influence of certain *rāgas* over nature that recall the legends of Orpheus and Apollo.

'Indian music can best be heard, and dancing seen, in the great southern cities such as Madura and Tanjore, and in the native states, Mysore and

Travancore. In such places it is still studied as a science by learned Brahmans and patronized by princes. You may engage a dancing girl and her musicians, and invite your friends; seated upon a carpet in a room bare of all furniture, your entertainment is more wonderful than any that money could buy in any other land; more wonderful at least for you, for it is one expression of that national culture of which you too are a part; it is your love and your emotion, your adoration for the Lord which the dancer dances and the singer sings. Another time she is to sing only for you; she brings a *tamburi* or a *vīṇā*, and seated like you upon the ground, pours out for as long as you will, songs of passionate love, or devotion moving you to tears.

Or it may be a man who plays or sings for you; one who has wandered from court to court and received the rewards of princes and kings. He plays the *sāraṅgī* as none else can; the Kashmir shawl he wears is the token of a raja's favour. There are no young men following in his steps; it is well to hear him while you may. In the north he will be perhaps a player on the *taus*, the 'peacock'. He too sings a song of passionate love, something at once so simple and so universal that it includes the love of God and the love of woman; it is part of the method of Indian poetry to carry double meanings, of which each deepens and explains the other, like the shot colours of a double-woven cloth. There are only four of you listening, and to-night you think only of devotion to the Lord, for that thought is in the singer's heart, and he is carried away by his own emotion and neither sees nor thinks of you. And yet if one in his heart thinks only of his beloved on earth, for him too is each love the symbol and revelation of the other.

> I am mad for my beloved: they say, what say they? Let them
> say what they will!
>
> Take me for a fool or a mad man; they say, what say they?
> Let them say what they will!
>
> I have nothing to do with them,
> Whether they be pleased with me or angry,
>
> May one only be gracious to me!
> They say, what say they? Let them say what they will!
>
> The Shaikh walks around his sanctuary;
> I offer up myself at thy altar,
>
> Call it sanctuary or hovel.
> They say, what say they? Let them say what they will!
>
> I have gazed on the glory and sheen of the cheeks of my beloved,
> I am burnt up as a moth in the flame,
>
> I am as one drunken:
> They say, what say they? Let them say what they will!

So simple is the cry; but it tells alike of the love of those great ones who 'are so enchanted with the beauty of the Creator of appearances, that they have nothing to do with the beauty of appearance itself', and of those with whom all the kingdoms of the earth weighs less than a feather in the scale against one woman only, upon whom their heart is set.

Even this is not the most wonderful experience which Indian music holds for those that have ears to hear. There is a music which comes once or twice only to you, and which it is vain to seek. The very greatest of Indian musicians are not professionals, but wandering holy men, players of the *taus* or *sāraṅgī* or *vīṇā*, or singers. Some evening in a northern town such a one passes by your door. You press him eagerly to lodge with you; if he will, to play for you; and he consents. You invite a few friends, and seated on the floor in an upper room, prepare to listen. A brass lamp burns by your side, and all is still. The player chooses an even simpler theme than the last,—'These many days I have not seen thee'. He sings and plays, and varies infinitely the expression of this one idea. He becomes almost a part of his instrument, and it and the sound of him. You lose consciousness of things external, and forget to move the wick, which burns dimly and more dimly still. As he plays on—'These many days I have not seen thee', this passionate cry materializes before your eyes as a dancing figure, it may be as the Lord Kṛṣṇa Himself, it may be as Rādhā, it may be in the form of one beloved on earth, whomsoever your thoughts are set upon, and to whom your love is given. You forget all else, and see only this rhythmic sweet appearance. At last the player ceases, leaving you silent and breathless, and the vision is gone like a dream. What did you see? You ask of one another, and you find that each saw before him his own thought, the one he loved best, and for whom in his heart was lamentation made,—'These many days I have not seen thee.'

Perhaps you are in the south. You have gone to a musical party, a wedding at the house of a friend, you are seated with many others on the cotton carpet, and before you is a band of drummers, oboists and players of the *vīṇā* and *tamburi*. A Brahman drums on an earthen pot. A slender girl of fifteen years sits demurely on the floor, dressed in silk brocade and golden chains, her feet and arms bare, and flowers in her hair. Her mother is seated near, back against the wall; she it is that trained the girl, and now she watches her proudly. The only sounds are those of the four strings of the ivory inlaid *tamburi* and the tapping of the drum. As you are waiting for the music to begin, a man with untidy hair and a saffron robe comes in, and your host gives him eager welcome, laying a white cloth on a stool for him to sit upon. All know him well—he is a sannyasi who wanders from temple to temple, preaching little, nor performing many ceremonies, but singing *tevarams* and the hymns of Manikka Vasagar. As he sits silent, all eyes are turned towards him, and conversation drops to a whisper. Presently he sings some hymn of passionate adoration of Śiva. His voice is thin but very sweet, melting the heart; his gentle strong personality holds every listener spellbound not least the little dancer to whom the words and music are so familiar; he is the dancer's and the drummers' friend and hero as much as yours. Some one asks for a special hymn, 'My God, why hast thou forsaken me?' and he sings.

Me, meanest one, in mercy mingling Thou didst make
  Thine own,
Lord of the Bull! Lo, thou'st forsaken me! O Thou
  who wear'st

Garb of fierce tiger's skin! Abiding Uttarakoça-
mangai's King!
Thou of the braided lock! I fainting sink. Our Lord,
uphold thou me!
What though I press no more the crimson lips of
maidens fair,
With swelling breasts; behold! Thou hast forsaken
me; though in,
Not out Thy worthy service, Uttarakoça-mangai's King,
I am! Though mad'st false me Thine own, why dost
Thou leave me now?[17]

Soon he rises, smiles at the musicians and speaks for a few moments with your host, and so goes away. And then you forget for a time this dreamer, in the beauty of the dance and the clamour of the drums. Of the dance you never weary; there is eternal wonder in the perfect refinement of its grace, and the mental concentration needed to control each muscle so completely; for this is not the passionate posturing born of a passing mood, but the elaborated art of three thousand years, an art that deceives you by its seeming simplicity, but in reality idealizes every passion, human and divine; for it tells of the intensity of Rādhā's love for Krishna. Rādhā was the leader of the herd-girls in Brindaban, and she, more than any, realised the depth and sweetness of the love of Krishna.[18]

Whatever place is held in the heart of Europe by the love of Dante for his Lady Beatrice, of Paolo for Francesca, of Deirdre for Naoisi, is held in India by the love stories of Rāma and Sītā, of Padmāvatī and Ratan Sen, and the love of Rādhā and Kṛṣṇa. Most wonderful of these was the love of Rādhā, in the absolute self-surrender of the human soul in her to the Divine in Kṛṣṇa is summed up all love. In this consecration of humanity there is no place for the distinction—always foreign to Indian thought—of sacred and profane. But when in love the finite is brought into the presence of the infinite, when the consciousness of inner and outer is destroyed in the ecstasy of union with one beloved, the moment of realization is expressed in Indian poetry, under the symbol of speech of Rādhā the leader of the Gopis with Kṛṣṇa the Divine Cowherd. And Kṛṣṇa is the Lord, Rādhā the soul that strives, in self-surrender, for inseparable oneness. 'And so both have told of the Lord,—the ascetic, for whom all earthly beauty is a vain thing, and the dancing girl, who is mistress of every art that charms the senses.

The music is to last all night; but you have to be home ere dawn, and as you pass along the road in the bright moonlight, you see that life, and the renunciation of life, lead both to the same goal at last. Both ascetic and musician shall be one Brahman with Himself; it is only a question of time, more, or less; and time, as every one knows, is unreal.

Oh Lord, look not upon my evil qualities!
Thy name, O Lord, is same-sightedness,
Make us both one Brahman.

This Hindu song of Sūrdās is said to have been sung by a dancing girl at a Rājpūt court. And there comes to you too the thought, that 'Whoso seeth all being in That One, and That in all, henceforth shall doubt no more.'

All this is passing away; when it is gone, men will look back on it with hungry dyes, as some have looked upon the life even of Mediaeval Europe, or of Greece. When civilization has made of life a business, it will be remembered that life was once an art; when culture is the privilege of bookworms, it will be remembered that it was once a part of life itself, not something achieved in stolen moments of relief from the serious business of being an engine-driver, a clerk, or a Governor.

Let those who are still part of such a life take note of it, that they may tell their children of it when it is nothing but a memory. A 'practical' and 'respectable' world has no place for the dreamer and the dancer; they belong to the old Hindu towns where the big temples and the *chatrams* tell of the faith and munificence of kings and merchant princes. In Madras there is the military band, or the music-hall company on tour,—what does it want with ascetics or with dancing girls?[19]

NOTES

1. Strabo, X. III.
2. Here the popular belief that the music of South India retains the ancient character of Indian music is reflected. This belief is now losing ground due to serious thinking in the last forty years or so. As for the resemblance of south Indian music to ancient Greek music, this point cannot be judged in isolation from the above.—Ed.
3. G. Lowes Dickinson, 'The Greek view of Life'.
4. This is a popular anecdote but the averseness of Aurangzeb to music has been challenged in recent researches (cf. Acharya Brhaspati, *Saṅgīta Cūḍāmaṇi*, part 1, p. 335, Sangeet Karyalaya, Hathras, 1976).—Ed.
5. Yoga Narendra Malla of Pālam (17th cent.) used on his coins the title Saṁgītārṇava-Pāraga, 'skilled in the sea of music'.
6. The last Nawab of Lucknow when deposed, brought many musicians and artists with him to Calcutta, where even now some of their descendants remain. The Nawab himself composed a song which is still often heard—*Jab se chora Lakhnav Nagar*, 'Now they have robbed me of Lucknow town.'
7. These passages are repeated from those of the preceding article, 'Indian Music'. —Ed.
8. C.R. Day, *Music and Musical Instruments of Southern India and the Deccan*, 1891.
9. *Ibid.*
10. C. Tirumalayya Naidu, *Asiatic Quarterly Review*, 1904, p. 117.
11. A.C. Wilson (Lady), *Short Account of the Hindu System of Music*, Lahore, 1904.
12. But *with the introduction of new signs and conventions*, it is not impossible to write down Indian music in staff notation.
13. Cheap harmoniums are now everywhere common in India.
14. Cf.: 'To avoid misunderstanding, it must be pointed out that by "a true record of a song" must not be understood once given variation of it, something fixed once for all. The accuracy or correctness of a record applies to most widely-differing

variations of one and the same song, and the greater the number of variations, the richer the material for comparative study, the easier it is to find out the most artistic specimen. A comprehensive collection of songs should contain different moments in the development of the same song, both as regards locality and time.' E. Lineff, *The Peasant Songs of Great Russia,* p. xiv.

15. See 'Music in East and West', by Maud MacCarthy, *Orpheus,* No. 3, 1908. This article is a valuable comparison of musical ideals and practice in East and West.
16. These passages occur in the previous essay 'Indian Music', also—Ed.
17. Adapted from the translation by Dr. Pope.
18. These passages are a repetition of those in the preceding article 'Indian Music'—Ed.
19. These passages are repeated from those in the preceding article, 'Indian Music'—Ed.

3. Music and Education in India*

In future years it is to be hoped . . . that the study of the national music of the country will occupy, as it should, a foremost place in all Indian Schools.

C.R. DAY, *Music and Musical Instruments of Southern India and the Deccan*, p. 7

The essential error in modern Indian education, as understood by Government, missionaries, and Anglicized Indians, is a refusal or inability to recognize any responsibility to the past. The consequent break in the continuity of the historical tradition is fatal to Indian culture. It is much as if the caretakers of some ancient building, of complex origin, and various ages, hitherto accustomed to make additions and enlargements where and when required, had suddenly abandoned this process of development, in order to pull down the whole building, with the intention of rebuilding it upon a new plan, with the result that most of their energies became occupied with the provision of temporary huts for the inhabitants of the old house thus turned out into the cold. While scarcely any time was thus left for the serious work of reconstruction, and the needs of the day continued to grow faster than ever before, it would not have been surprising if some of the builders and their critics had regretted their haste in abandoning the old building, and reflected that their labours would have been better directed in building a new wing worthy of the old, than in pulling down what already existed. This is in fact just what is happening in India today; the destructive rather than constructive character of much of the education given in Indian schools and colleges is being recognized, but so slowly, that it is an open question whether any part of the old structure can be saved, to witness that the ancient builders builded well.

Take music as a single case. The importance of music in education could hardly be overestimated. 'Is not', says Plato,

> education in music of the greatest importance, because that the measure and harmony enter in the strongest manner into the inward part of the soul. . . . The man who hath here been educated as he ought, perceives in the quickest manner whatever workmanship is defective, and whatever execution is unhandsome, or whatever productions are of that kind; and being disgusted in a proper manner, he will praise what is beautiful, rejoicing in it and receiving it into his soul, be nourished by it, and become a worthy and good man. Education in music is for the sake of such things as these.

*A.K. Coomaraswamy, *Essays in National Idealism*, Colombo, 1909.

These words a modern Welsh writer does but echo when he says:

Rightly studied, music has all the exactness of pure reason and science, all the expansiveness of the imaginative reason, all the metaphysic of the profoundest philosophy, and the ethic of the purest religion in it. . . . It is an energy of the mind in the first instance, and is of incalculable advantage in obtaining dominion over the body. . . . Music, properly taught, includes all that is generally conceded to belong to a liberal education.[1]

These ideas are far more clearly recognizable in Indian than in English culture. But English education, as hitherto imparted and understood in India, has merely ignored the importance of music and art in education. There is in India no educational institution under European guidance where Indian music has any place whatever in the scheme of education. There is no Indian university where Indian music is recognized.[2] Of Europeans engaged in education in India, it is safe to say that not 1 per cent have any knowledge of Indian music as a science, or appreciation of it as an art. The majority frankly regard it as so much noise. This is only one instance, but a typical one, of the unfitness of Englishmen to control Indian education; they are unfitted alike by lack of knowledge and by lack of sympathy. The only place for English teachers in India today, whatever it may have been in the past, is in the employ of Indian educationalists, to whom alone they should be responsible. They should be engaged only for special purposes, as in Japan, and should not be allowed to control in matters concerning the aim of method of education as a whole. The control of Indian education is of so much importance that the necessity of gaining this would alone justify the present endeavour to attain political freedom.

Indian girls are often taught to play the piano in English schools, especially in Mission schools.[3] The only result of this is that they lose the power of appreciating their own melodies; their execution scarcely ever reaches a high level; they cannot afford so expensive an instrument as a good piano in afterlife; and they despise the inferior taste of their parents and companions at home, who understand Indian music, and for whom European music is meaningless. A writer on Scottish song has remarked, in words most applicable to India:

I have often wondered if the introduction of the cheap piano has anything to do with the decline of song as a means of expression amongst the people. Before the era of universal piano playing, the people used to think music; and from thinking to expressing is but a step . . . now their ambition is to have a piano[4] and to have their children learn to play. 'Learning music' to them means learning to play the piano, and so that unfortunate instrument has become to them, as to the vast majority, a substitute for music in the brain . . . many . . . think it a mark of inferiority to confess acquaintance with their own songs when they can have English music and a piano.[5]

Music in fact, is contemplated in modern 'English' education in India by no means as an energy of the mind, but essentially as an accomplishment; and it is in the vast majority of cases only as an accomplishment that European music can be taught in India.

The introduction to India of the piano, and Western music generally, is sometimes defended on the plea that both types may be 'enjoyed'.[6] The superficiality of this view is evident;—as if the origin and purpose of music were but 'amusement'. *Music and art are not amusements invented by idle men to pass away the time of other idlers; they are expansions of personality, essential to true civilization, expressions of the human spirit, confirming the sincere conviction that man does not live by bread alone.* Music, even more than plastic art, is a function of the higher consciousness. The true musician is the Keltic harper who hears the music of the fairies, or the Indian singer who hears the voices of gandharvas. Only such, like Gutilla, can call angels down from heaven. I heard of one living singer at Tanjore, who had no voice or power to sing, but longed to express devotion to the Lord in music: he called upon Sarasvatī, and like Caedmon, his lips were opened. This true music is as exalted as its source. All great art is truly of supersensuous origin. If art and music are thus expressions, manifestations, it is obvious that the result of imitation and borrowing of the natural modes of expression belonging to other nations whose idiosyncracy and environment are different, must be disastrous; and in point of fact, the attempt to replace Indian by Western music in India, results only in vulgarization,—that essential vulgarization which, as Ruskin remarks, consists in not understanding the effect produced by the imitation.

There may be some whose broad culture enables them truly to appreciate the music evolved by temperaments and in environments so different as those of East and West. There must necessarily be few, and meanwhile the standard of Western music in India is set by those altogether out of touch with it, a bourgeois public satisfied with gramophones. One thing is certain, that a pretence at the same time of despising Indian and of admiring European music is for a true Indian ridiculous. Western culture may be, and will be, of value to the East, but it must be as a postgraduate course—it will not stand in the place of mother milk. *We cannot understand others by ceasing to understand ourselves.*

Pierre Loti in his book on India, describes the music which he heard in Travancore. The Maharajah's musicians had been playing. 'This orchestra', he says, 'and these singers belong to the Maharajah. . . . How far away this prince's dreams must be from ours, how different his conceptions of the sorrows that belong to love and death. But this exquisite and rare music of his, reveals to me something of his soul, something that I should never see in our short and formal interviews, burdened with ceremony and foreign words.' Now mark the effect of the introduction of European music at such a court; the Raja replaces his group of skilled musicians, whose music even to a stranger is in some measure an interpretation of the national genius, by a newly trained brass band, the performances of which may, with good fortune, rival those of a third rate German band in England. The Raja buys also gorgeous gramophones and a mechanical violin, paying fabulous sums to have them decorated by their English manufacturers. The true artistes of the past he neglects; the hereditary craftsmen, makers of exquisite inlaid and painted lutes and marvellous drums, are left to starve; and to the cultured stranger it can but seem that his must have been an inferior race, with little learning and few traditions worth preserving, for he finds there no new revelation of humanity, only a distorted image of himself.

Quite possibly such a Raja is at the same time 'progressive' and 'enlightened'. He spends money on 'female' education; adopts the Resident's suggestions of founding a museum, or the like, and believes himself to be all that he can or should be. There can be few more depressing sights than that of such men destroying with one hand what they endeavour to build up with the other.

Suppose, for the sake or argument, that one were to admit a superiority of harmony to melody, of European to Indian music. It would be much as if we should say that Greek architecture was superior to Gothic, or *vice versa,* instead of recognizing that each is the expression of a different temperament in relation to different environment and different needs; but let that pass, and ask even on this assumption of superiority what does and must result from an endeavour to introduce European music into India at the cost of Indian.

The comprehension of harmony, especially of its later developments, is even in Europe necessarily confined to those who have had an elaborate musical education, more particularly intellectual than emotional. Only those, moreover, who can afford to pay the cost of expensive concerts, can often hear this highly elaborated music. *But in India music is not only for the wealthy virtuoso; it is a part of the national life, it is still an art, not an accomplishment or an intellectual exercise; the music of India is found in the hearts of the people.* Rob them of this, by setting up a false standard of 'correctness', and in a hundred years, how many Indians will have learnt to appreciate elaborate harmonies, or even have the opportunity of hearing European music adequately performed? Probably not one in ten thousand. At the same time, the possibility of creative expression, now common amongst Indian musicians, must die out; for it is not easier to use a foreign musical language than to use a foreign literary speech. So long, in fact, as education is founded upon a foreign culture, you can only produce 'accomplishments' and impart 'useful information'; you cannot give the means of creative self-expression, possible only in the mother-tongue, whether of speech or song.

And if, in a hundred years, some slight acquaintance with European harmonized music should be acquired by a small section of the community, how many will have forgotten in that time the refinement and vitality of their own melodies, and have turned instead to the gramophone and cheap harmonium, or whatever more vulgar mechanical devices may by then have been invented? Almost all will have so forgotten and so turned away, for it is the gramophone and the harmonium, and the cheap ill-taught piano, that stand in India for European music.

It is certain then, that, while the importance of music in education can hardly be overrated, such education must be primarily an education in Indian music, if it is to have any value as a discipline or as an art, or in any more serious sense than as a mere accomplishment. *This is not to say that Indian music must not change or be influenced in any way by changed conditions; but that such change must be organic, not sudden, and that it must be an evolution in accordance with the bent of the national genius.* In all education schemes, music must be taken into account as a part of everyday life. Religious songs, songs of agriculture and the crafts, of the love of the land, folk songs must be heard in every school.

In hundreds of Indian schools under more or less direct British control, the only musical education received today is the annual singing of a bad translation of the English National Anthem. All this is puerile. The object of education must be to make good Indian citizens, and this can only be effected by using the national culture and the national languages—literary, musical, artistic—as the medium of instruction.

In all these respects, music is but the type of every factor in culture and education. The people's intelligence can be developed primarily only by means of education in the national culture. One must learn to understand that with which they are already familiar before it is possible to understand the unfamiliar, and relate it to one's own life. Only vulgarity can result from imitating what one does not so understand and cannot so relate to one's own individuality. The first necessity in India today is National Education.

Music has sometimes been divided into two kinds, folk music and art music, much as art is sometimes classified into decorative and fine. Both distinctions are half-truths, and sometimes obscure the deeper fact that all art has a fundamental unity. But, accepting the distinction as a temporary convenience, it may be remarked that, in spite of the neglect of Indian art music in recent times, the folk music of the people is still everywhere to be heard, and it is only in a living relation to this that a national school of music can be preserved. The attempt to denationalize Indian music by learning European music instead is the sure way to an extinction of the musical faculty, comparable to that which took place in England after the time of Charles I. This decadence coincided with the day when no gentleman's education was considered complete until he had made the 'grand tour' on the continent—and returned from it to turn up his nose, as the Rev. S. Baring Gould remarks, at his old English Manor house, and to call in Italian architects to tear it down and substitute for it a Florentine Palazzo. This is what English-educated and 'England-returned' Indians are doing in India today.

As a matter of fact no School of Music has arisen and flourished in Modern Europe that has not been founded on National folk music, and been concerned with the expression of national aspirations and ideals. Russia may be taken as an example. The founder of the Russian School was Glinka (1803-57) who was called by List the 'Prophet-Patriarch' of Russian music. He grew up steeped in the folk music of his own country, and early in life, conceived the idea of composing a national opera. This ambition he eventually satisfied in 'The Life of the Tsar' (1836), an opera which marked an epoch in the musical history of Russia. As Mrs. Newmarch has said:[7]

> The more thoughtful critics saw that the opera was now in the best sense of the word, and marked a fresh departure in Art—the will of a genuine school of Russian

music. . . . He did not merely play with local colour, but recast the primitive speech of the folk-song into a new and polished idiom, so that henceforth Russian music was able to take its place among the distinctive schools of Western Europe.

India may learn from England's experience. From the age of Purcell to the present day, the music of England has been essentially foreign—Italian, German, Russian, Hungarian, but not English. 'The question now to be considered' says a writer quoted above 'is whether English music is capable of resuscitation. One thing is certain; the present vogue of training English musicians to lisp in the tongue of the foreigner can have no beneficial outcome. It is emphatically not that way that salvation lies.'[8] It was long believed that the English people were actually unmusical, and that there were amongst them no folk songs, comparable to those of other European nations, the foundation of their schools of national music. This opinion has proved in recent times erroneous; a vast body of English folk song still exists, and is known to the last generation of country folk, though the present generation is generally scornful of the old songs. It is however, with the true folk music that the hope of a School of English music rests. The movement for the teaching of folk music as a part of all educational schemes is growing stronger daily. Its importance has long been recognized in other countries, as Denmark and Hungary.

As Mr. Sharp remarks, the spectacle of a great progressive nation like England, 'intent upon the instruction of her people in their own folk-songs', gathered, very often, from the lips of illiterate peasants is a strange one. And yet, if in India we have no more love for our own music than England had in the early nineteenth century, we too must pass through a long epoch of barrenness and formalism, before we awaken to the fact that we have neglected the one thing vital, that is the music living in the hearts of peasants, uneducated and illiterate—but more truly Indian than their 'educated' 'superiors'. We too, in time to come, shall be intent upon the instruction of the people in their own folk songs.[9] *Would it not be wiser to bethink ourselves in time, to save what is with us now, instead of making so needlessly hard the task of those that will come after us, and so needlessly barren our own lives and the lives of those who like some of us have not understood?*

These are the days of nation building. Yet how many 'nationalists' are in truth 'denationalists' in their lives and aspirations! They want to be 'free', to compete with Europe on her own lines, to be 'progressive', 'advanced', to gain political power and material success. It is not with these that the future of India lies. It lies in the lives of those who are truly Indian at heart, whose love for India is the love of a lover for his mistress, who believe that India still is (and not merely may be, when duly 'educated') the light of the World, who today judge all things by Indian standards, and in whom is manifest the work of the shapers of India from the beginning until now. Without these, there can be no Indian future worth the name. How may they be known? Like answers unto like; but, if an empirical test be asked for, I believe that the love of Indian music and the comprehension of Indian art are tests unfailing.

The direct results of making Indian music an essential part of the educational ideal may be many and various. We have already seen that a proper education in music is everywhere recognized as an invaluable aid in the training of character—the true aim of education. But some aspects of the results may be noted in greater detail. There can be no true patriotism without patriotic education. The primary aim of education in India should be the production of Indian citizens. No Indian can be a true citizen of the world, except by being first an Indian citizen, and from that standpoint entering into the life of humanity outside of India. This however is not the time for cosmopolitanism, it is the time when India herself needs Indian citizens; and education in Indian music is an essential part of education in Indian citizenship, whether for those who may never learn a word of English or see even a Raja's brass band, but are more Indian at heart than many of those whose false education has brought so much that is vulgar, so much that is unlovely into the life of modern India, or for those whose life-work leads them into other lands, to bear the message of the East, or to become intellectual parasites, as the case may be. In schools then, Indian folk music must be taught as a matter of course—religious, agricultural and craft songs, and songs of the love of the land—not forgetting 'Bande Mataram'. These songs must be orally taught, or to a drum or *tambur* accompaniment only, not to the piano. To older students the really quite simple theoretical part of Indian music should be taught, as European musical theory is taught in European schools. The result of this education in taste will be that, as the boys and girls grow up, they will be in a position to understand and care for the most highly developed art music of India.

In almost all cases, it will be found that Oriental art, and music and literature have been produced for audiences far more cultivated, in respect of imagination and sympathy, than the audiences appealed to by the artist and musician in the modern West. A great part of this cultivation depended on the existence of a common national culture, in which all shared in the measure of their capacity. The result of this is that the artist in his art relies on his audience to understand refinements and suggestions which now are not understood by reason of the divorce of education from the real life and desires of the people. Hence it is that the 'educated' of today have lost their love of Indian music, and find amusement in gramophone They are no more able to understand real Indian music than the frequenter of London music halls could understand Greek drama. The restoration of Indian folk and art music to its proper place in Indian education will alter this, and restore the necessary attitude of mind, the preparation, which are required to understand the self expression of India in her music.

How exactly opposite the result at present attained can be, the following episode, only too typical, will illustrate. Not long ago a relation of my own, mother of many children, well educated, and understanding Tamil, some Sanskrit, and English, sang for me certain Tamil and Sanskrit songs. Meanwhile her son, who was then a student at a Government College where his own language, and much more his own music, was ignored and despised, continued to work a gramophone, showing neither any appreciation of the Indian songs, or any respect for mother or guest. If 'civilisation' be the production of, in the best sense, civil persons, how had it failed here! I have met also many who have been ashamed of their own music, even of their own language. The same results may be seen, depending on the same causes, in Scotland and Ireland. Ireland has had the strength to react in time, and renationalize her education, as far as might be in the face of educational authorities quite as unimaginative as those we are familiar with in India. The only hope in India lies in a control of education by Indians.

Another direct result of the present neglect of Indian music in education is what I may call the boycott of Indian musical instrument makers in favour of manufacturers of gramophones and harmoniums. This fact, further elaborated on p. 160,[10] I present to workers in the Swadeshi movement for due consideration in all its ramifications and parallels.

Education in Indian music, that is, education in folk music in elementary schools, will make possible the education of older boys and girls, and young men and women, who possess musical talent, in the art music of India, song, the *vīṇā*, the *sāraṅgi*. The advantage of these over more mechanical instruments lies in the fact that only the truly musical can master them. A gramophone, and even a piano, often enables the most unmusical person to inflict a suffering audience with his ideas. It is true some efforts have been made by Indians in recent years to provide for education in Indian music, and some of these may be briefly noticed. The Gayan Samaj in Poona and Madras; the Academy of Music in Calcutta, founded by Raja Sir S.M. Tagore, Mus. D. (Oxon.); the Bengal Music School in Calcutta; schools in the Central Provinces; individual teachers such as the *ustad* of Baroda, court musicians of the Gaekwar, and others: all these by their publications and through their pupils have contributed to the preservation of Indian music. But the influence of even these schools is not always certain. One of the most important is the Gandharva Maha Vidyalaya, or Indian Musical College in Lahore, founded in 1901, for the 'revival of ancient Hindu music and its diffusion among the general public'. It is a musical college with a variety of courses, extending over periods from six months to two years in extent. The learned principal is assisted by six other pandits. But even here the decline of true Indian music was to be remarked. When I visited the college in 1907, I found 14 boys learning the harmonium, and one only the *vīṇā*, the classical and best instrument of India. One wonders how any college professing to teach *Indian* music can allow a harmonium within its doors. They told me it was so easy—in three months you can play a tune on it, and earn money at weddings and other entertainments. It is said that the *vīṇā* takes sixty years to learn, and it is hard to find ten more to play it in. Assuredly the harmonium *is* easy, it does not require musical talent, merely a little, very little, perseverance. It is above all easy as played in India; the player attempts no harmonies (wisely perhaps), but picks out a mere succession of notes, the bare skeleton of some Hindustani air, omitting lesser intervals and cadence; or an English music hall ditty. Yes, it is easy. Is not that the secret, or one of the secrets of the degeneration of

Indian taste? It is easier to boil your cloth in an aniline dye, than to spend months in producing a beautiful and permanent colour; easier to pick out notes on a harmonium than to play the *vīṇā* or violin; easier to subscribe for shares in a Swadeshi factory than to re-organize and support a village industry; easier to drift than to swim. But for India, is it worthwhile, is this the Art of Living? Is not an India thus subdued in soul more lost than any India governed by the sword could be?

One cannot gather grapes of thorns; you cannot in the long run get something for nothing. Do not let us pretend that it is possible. If our ideal is one of purely material prosperity, and we have no time for music or the arts, let us have done with them altogether; but if we think that music and the arts belong to the most significant, the most real part of our lives, let us cherish them accordingly. Let us decide; but in either case do not let us pretend that the harmonium and the gramophone are compensations for Indian music. It is not possible for anything to be a compensation for the loss of Indian music.

NOTES

1. D. Frangcon Davies, in *Wales To-day and To-morrow*, 1907.
2. See note 1 on p. 24.
3. In many such schools they are taught to sing to a 'baby organ' or harmonium, instruments which, in comparison to Indian instruments, are related much as the stream organ of an English fair is related to the music of Purcell and William Byrd. Few things, too, can be more sad than the waste of faculty involved in the teaching of European scales and songs to children who are capable of using the more elaborate and varied scales of the East.
4. In modern India more frequently the cheap harmonium.
5. Helen Hopekirk, *Seventy Scottish Songs*, Boston, 1905.
6. The word being used in the limited sense of gratification or amusement.
7. *Grove's Mus. Dict.* Ed. II, 180-8.
8. C.J. Sharp, *English Folk Song*, 1907.
9. In speaking of folk music in India, it must be understood that there is not in India that divorce between folk music and art music which, like the distinction between decorative and fine art, is so unfortunate a feature of European culture. The folk music of India, is the music of all the folk, and really includes the highest forms of 'art' music.
10. The passage referred to here has been reproduced on pages 16-17 of this volume. —Ed.

4. Gramophones—and why not?*

The present age is often—and correctly—described, as an age of mechanism. For nearly a century, scientific discoveries have been utilized with unprecedented rapidity and success, in making life faster and more comfortable, and in increasing the available sum of concrete knowledge. There are no limits to the possible extension of this process, except in a reaction, of which traces are already recognizable, against the intrusion of the Frankenstein of mechanism upon domains to which he should never have been admitted. *For surely mechanism must be for man, not man for mechanism, and man sooner or later will revolt against his own slavery.*

Meanwhile, the discovery of each new mechanical device, and of each new method of 'conquering nature'—as the stupid phrase runs—is hailed as self-evident proof of progress. With every fresh 'scientific miracle' the self-conceit of a sensation-and-comfort-loving public rises higher.

Yet it is more than possible that later ages will look back upon the present period as one of peculiar blindness in respect of the realities. *For a society which sees wealth and progress in things rather than in men must sooner or later stand condemned.*

In the present paper I do not intend to treat at any length of the relation of mechanism to industry. It is well to remember, however, that the promise of mechanism has not yet been fulfilled. So far from 'saving labour' for the worker, its chief results have mostly been increased possibility of profit-making for manufacturers, and the replacement of quality by quantity as the means of successful trade. Simultaneously there has been accomplished the degradation of the worker from the level of an intelligent craftsman to that of a living machine. Just how this process works may be illustrated by the following slightly adapted extract from the preface to my '*Mediaeval Sinhalese Art*:

> Not merely is the workman through division of labour no longer able to make any whole thing, not only is he confined to making small parts of things, but it is impossible for him to improve his position or to win reward for excellence in the craft itself. Under guild conditions it was possible and usual for the apprentice to rise through all grades of knowledge and experience to the position of a master-craftsman. But take any such trade as weaving[1] under modern conditions by power loom. The operator has no longer to design or weave in and out the threads with his own fingers or to throw the shuttle with his own hand. He is employed, in reality, not as a weaver, but as the tender of a machine. . . . That craft is for him destroyed as a means of culture, and the community has lost one more man's intelligence for it is obviously futile to attempt to build up by evening classes and free libraries what the whole of a man's work is for

* A.K. Coomaraswamy, *Essays in Indian Idealism*, Colombo, 1909.

ever breaking down. It is no longer possible for culture and refinement to come to the craftsman through his work; they must be won, if won at all, in spite of his work; he must seek them in a brief hour snatched from rest and sleep, at the expense of life itself. . . . There can be no quality of leisure in his work. In short, *commercial production absolutely forbids a union of art with labour.*

In the words of Ruskin, 'Industry without art is Brutality.' Yet it should not be thought that the recognition of these facts involves a wholesale attack upon every form of mechanism, or an impossible desire to revert absolutely to mediaeval conditions. Mechanism has come to stay, and has its due purpose to serve as a hewer of wood and drawer of water. *But it is for man to see that his servant does not become his master.* That is to say, a discrimination must be made between the legitimate and illegitimate functions of machinery in industry. I do not propose to speak further of this part of the subject here; but this much at least is clear, that the multiplication of unskilled labour which results from the complete subordination of the craftsman to the machine is injurious to the national quality. *Ceteris paribus*, a handicraft is always preferable to a mechanical industry.

The immediate object of this paper, however, is briefly to treat of the relation of mechanism to art, as typified in the relation of the gramophone to music.

Whatever the relation of mechanism to industry, it should be self-evident that it can have no real relation to art. The non-relation of mechanism to art will need no proof to the man who, in Plato's words, 'hath here been educated as he ought, and perceives in the quickest manner whatever workmanship is defective, and whatever execution is unhandsome'. It is significant, moreover, that it was through education in music that Plato would have attained this very end, that one should, while still young and 'before he is able to understand reason', instinctively know what is to be praised and received into the soul, and what is to be despised and rejected. This is the highest understanding, to know without reasoning what is worthy or unworthy. For those who have this understanding, 'reasonable proof' is superfluous, and at the same time difficult.

Let us, however, consider the gramophone. It provides, you say, innocent entertainment for all. It will be found that this statement needs considerable qualification. In the first place, to a person of culture—especially musical culture—the sound of a gramophone is not an entertainment, but the refinement of torture. The combination in one person of a highly developed musical taste, and of pleasure in the sound of a gramophone could hardly be imagined. Above all, those who are themselves musicians understand what a blunting of sensibilities is indicated in the acceptance of the gramophone approximation as a substitute for music. The more often and more fully you are pleased and satisfied by this approximation, the more the finer musical sensibilities are dulled. So much for the audience—the effect is to degrade the standard of appreciation.

'Ah, you have never heard a good gramophone', I am often told. This mythical instrument I never expect to hear. But let us suppose, by way of meeting all possible eventualities,[2] that a gramophone is available which even a musician cannot distinguish from the real thing. Which is to be desired in a community, the possession of musicians, or of machines that can amuse us? Do we desire men, or things? Every time you accept a gramophone in place of a man you degrade the musician, take from him his living, and injure the group-soul of your people. So it appears that your amusement is not quite so innocent as it appeared.

But to return to the audience—do you really think that the most perfect machine can take the place of a living singer or player? The performance of a musician is never exactly repeated—on each occasion he adapts himself insensibly to the different conditions, and finds also in himself new expression through the old form. There is moreover his personal influence, the power of his personality, the vision of a living man giving expression to emotions in a disciplined traditional art language. For pure hideousness and lifelessness on the other hand few objects could exceed a gramophone. The more decorated it may be, the more its intrinsic ugliness is revealed.[3]

Again, musical instruments such as a *vīṇā, sitār* or *sāraṅgī* have each their own individuality, they possess an individual temperament which the artist must understand and with which he can co-operate. The more such an instrument is played on, the richer it becomes in association, and the more it will be valued by the musician. The manufacture of such instruments is a means of culture to the craftsman; not so the mechanical production of the various parts of a gramophone or harmonium in great factories, where each part is made by a different man, and the whole put together by another.

The intervention of mechanism between the musician and the sound is always, *per se*, disadvantageous. The most perfect music is that of the human voice. The most perfect instruments are those stringed instruments where the musician's hand is always in contact with the string producing the sound, so that every shade of his feeling can be reflected in it. Even the piano is relatively an inferior instrument, and still more the harmonium, which is only second to the gramophone as evidence of the degradation of musical taste in India.

One great disadvantage of mechanical instruments is the fatal facility they afford to the undisciplined and untrained mind to attempt the work of the true musician. A few rupees spent on a gramophone, a few months spent in playing with one finger on a harmonium, and the half educated philistine of today is prepared to dispense with the services of the interpreters of national music, disciplined by years of study and training to the expression of the highest ideals of the race consciousness.

It will be seen that the use of the harmonium is only in a degree less vicious. Easy to learn, it degrades popular taste almost as effectively as the gramophone displaces the trained musician, and destroys the true character of Indian music, and the voice-quality even of the trained musician who makes use of it. These two instruments, if care be not taken, will in a few years more complete the vulgarization of Indian music.

The highest ideal of nationality is that of service. India, by the scorn which she has cast upon her own arts, by the degradation of standard in her own culture, here sufficiently evidenced by the possibility of finding pleasure in a gramophone or a harmonium, is casting aside this highest privilege of service. Nations are judged not by what they assimilate, but by what they contribute to human culture. India, by her blindness to the beauty that till yesterday was everywhere in and around her in art and music, is forfeiting this privilege of service. For no man of another nation will come to learn of India, if her teachers be gramophones and harmoniums and imitators of European realistic art.

NOTES

1. I have here substituted 'weaving' for the original 'carpet-making', as no carpets are made on power-looms in India at present, and the problem as it concerns weaving is actually before us.
2. As a matter of fact, the eventuality considered is really impossible because it is not the principle of the gramophone to reproduce the original sound, but to produce vibration sufficiently near to the original one to have a similar effect.
3. It should be understood that the condemnation of the gramophone here given is concerned solely with its use as a substitute for music as an art. Just as machinery has a due place in industry, so even the gramophone has a use. This use is however as a scientific instrument—not as an interpreter of human emotion. In the recording of songs, the analysis of music for theoretical purposes, and especially, perhaps, in the exact study of an elaborate melody of Indian music, the gramophone has a place. This however is work for the few, and, so far from this use being recognized hitherto, we have had merely the abuse and not the use before us.

5. Classic *Rāgs**

It is necessary that the reader should have some idea of the meaning of the word *rāga* or *rāg*. Originally meaning 'passion', 'emotion', the word as used in Indian music applies to certain combinations of notes which form the bare skeleton out of which a song is made. Each of these combinations of notes, called a *rāg*, has an appropriate time of day and sentiment associated with it, expressed by, and inseparable from it; in other words, quite definite emotions and even external physical effects, are associated by the Indians, as by the ancient Greeks, with particular combinations of sounds, which are therefore called *rāgs*. Learning to sing or play Indian music consists in learning to improvise in various *rāgs*. To be called a musician at all requires this: so that while the Western printed-song may be compared to a poem for recitation, the Indian taught-song is a theme variously elaborated by each musician and on each occasion, never exactly repeated. Those are highly praised who can improvise at great length in a given *rāg* without obvious repetitions. All musicians are expected to be able to sing or play in a good number of *rāgs*, while on the other hand there are very many *rāgs*, but little known and hardly ever used. Theoretically a *rāg* is absolutely fixed; but even when the same name persists across wide areas, slight changes in the notes are sometimes recognizable, though the character of the whole remains unchanged. It is expected of any good patron of music, that, beside understanding the various times employed, he should be able to recognize the *rāgs* used, and to detect the introduction of any extraneous note not proper to the *rāg* in use. One who would pronounce any technical criticism on Indian music, based on the actual music and not merely on sound-quality or other element varying with the performer, must acquire at least this minimum of knowledge.

The word *rāg* in Indian music, may be translated as 'melody-mould' or 'musical pattern'. A *rāg* is not a scale, but is made up of from five to seven notes selected from the Indian scale of 22 notes. A *rāg* is not a mode, for it is more than a mere selection of notes: it is an outline pattern, in which such notes, and only such notes, are used. There can be no accidentals in a strict *rāg*. A *rāg* has nothing to do with a key: for the singer, however many *rāgs* he may use, keeps his *tambura* invariably tuned at the same pitch, suiting his voice.

The simplest form of a *rāg* is called its *taswīr* or 'picture'. This is first taught, forming a 'trunk' to which 'leaves and branches' can afterwards be added. *Taswīrs* of the nine *rāgs* illustrated here, are given together before the musical examples, for comparison, beginning with the pentatonics and following in order of completeness and complexity. This is not the order in

* Introduction to A.K. Coomaraswamy's *Thirty Songs from Panjab and Kashmir*, 1912; rpt. New Delhi, 1994.

which the *rāgs* are taught: Bhairavī, as the easiest, is taught first, while Kāndra, Behāg, and Mālkaus are reckoned very difficult.

From what has been said, it will be seen that the records given here must represent, not the only rendering, but a typical rendering of the songs. The songs were first learnt by imitation, and studied until they could be sung to the *ustād's* satisfaction, no easy matter, by reason of the extraordinary elusiveness of Indian songs when first heard, and the exacting standard of the teacher. Only after the song had thus been learnt, was an attempt made to write out a complete version in staff notation, although, of course, notes were made all the time. I believe that this way of slavish imitation is the only, or at any rate, the best way in which Indian music be seriously studied by Europeans; only after learning oneself to sing, is it possible to completely analyse what is sung. It may be possible at a later stage, when a new notation is further evolved, to do more directly analytical work; but nothing can remove the necessity for noting many versions and variations, and for remembering that the printed result indicates only how a song should be sung, not the exact form to be followed upon every occasion.

In these respects the classic music here recorded, differs from the Kāshmīrī folk songs given in Part II. These, like folk songs in India proper, are much less variable than the classical music; the air is often exactly repeated verse after verse, and on separate occasions, and can thus be written down directly from the original singer.

In reading the music given here in Part I, being examples of *ustādī* songs in nine *rāgs*, it is absolutely necessary to keep in mind the following points if serious error is to be avoided.

The scale is just, and will be falsified if the notes are played on any keyed instrument. They should be simply read, vocalized, or played on a violin or cello. None of the songs is written in a key, and the sharps and flats indicated must not be taken as equivalent to a key signature. The various songs are written down so as to come but within the compass of an ordinary voice, the note corresponding to *sa* being indicated in each case: but the *taswīrs* are written with G = *sa* in all cases, for convenience of comparison. The bars indicate only the rhythmic structure: accent does not necessarily fall on the first of the bar as written.

The best guide to singing will be found in the phrasing and marked accents. It would rarely be possible to exaggerate the *portamento*. As regards the words, it will suffice for most purposes to pronounce the vowels and consonants as in Italian, care being taken to fully utter doubled and aspirated consonants.

Syllables forming part of one word are connected by continuous lines: last syllables of words to be held on are indicated by dots. Syllables interpolated in singing, are printed in italics.

Abdul Rahīm. A few words must be said about our *ustād*, Abdul Rahīm of Kapurthala. Between him and Devī there was formal acceptance of the relation of teacher and pupil, with all due solemnity and offerings. Thereafter

Abdul Rahīm came with us for about ten weeks to Kāshmīr, and Devī studied daily, until State orders recalled him from his period of leave, to Kapurthala, where he is a State-pensioned *kalānt*. His ancestors were Brāhmans, forcibly converted in the time of Aurangzeb. Like many other Panjābī Musulmāns in the same case, the family retain many Hindu customs, e.g., non-remarriage of widows. Abdul Rahīm's faith in Hindu gods is as strong as his belief in Islam and Moslem saints, and he sings with equal earnestness of Kṛṣṇa or Allah, exemplifying the complete fusion of Hindu and Moslem tradition characteristic of so many pārts of northern India today. He is devout and even superstitious; he would hesitate to sing Dīpak *Rāg*, unless in very cold weather. He is foresighted and has prophetic dreams, and like his father Aliyās who served the Jodhpur court, is something of *fakīr*. Slight and delicate, gentle-mannered and patient, an inveterate smoker of *hookah*, a first rate teacher, a great boaster, much too fond of presents and too ready to ask for them, a true artist and often unmistakably inspired, finding his art now less and less appreciated, yet conscious of the dignity of his inherited skill—such are the salient characteristics of a rather pathetic figure, not without nobility, but such as the Board school education of Indian universities finds little use for.

Abdul Rahīm has a profound knowledge of many classical *rāgs* and some folk songs, which last he will only sing under protest; he has a sweet, but not very strong voice which he frequently overstrains, and accompanies with expressive, but sometimes too violent gesticulation. His songs are in various dialects and languages: Panjābī, Dogrī, Urdu, Hindī, Sindī, Persian, Arabic.

Words. If we consider the words of the songs, we find that they fall into two sections, a folk and a literary group. The only pure folk song of which words and music are given here, is the short song in Chamba Pahārī: but the other Pahārī is clearly folk song more embroidered, and the words of many more of his songs belong to the folk (e.g. 'Lachhi', 'Death', etc.).

The motifs of the other songs are literary and religious: some in various ways Moslem (many Sufī), and others Vaiṣṇava, or like the beautiful *Āpe āye* (musical example No. 11) almost unsectarian.

The words of many art songs resemble those of purely folk-origin in being anonymous and traditionally handed down in varying versions. It must always be difficult to draw a definite line between folk and art song in a country like India, where the greatest works of literature have been so long orally transmitted, and no complete method of musical notation exists, where also, the most essential part of any real education has been always held to be the teacher, and not the mere facts imparted. No doubt, as in Europe, the adoption of notation and extended use of writing and printing for music and song-words, will lead to a more definite divergence between folk and art music than at present appears. Now, broadly speaking, we may say as regards words, that those are of the folk whose motifs are naive and local, whose rhythm is very definite, where refrains are characteristic, the language popular and the number of verses large. As regards tunes, those of the folk are the more definite, admitting of less variation than those of art songs: often they are not in a definite *rāg*, or if in a *rāg*, then sung in a set form not admitting of *ad libitum* variation.

Alāp. In art songs, the language and motifs are more or less literary, and the words confined to a single couplet, or at most a couple of four-line stanzas: the words are made entirely subservient to the music, sometimes serving as little more than syllables for vocalization. In the *alāps*, the most advanced form of art song, words are altogether dispensed with, meaningless syllables being used for vocalization.[1] These *alāps* are not in strict time, and so not accompanied by the drummer, except for a moment here and there where the rhythm becomes definite: but they are often followed by a song in the same *rāg* in strict time. Thus, the beautiful Behāg alāp of musical example No. 3 may be followed without pause by the much more rapid and lively 'Gopī's Complaint' of example No. 4. The *alāp* itself could, of course, be indefinitely extended. The syllables used in vocalization are *ā, na, nuṅ, ri,* etc.

Hard as it would be to choose among the many wonderful songs we have heard our *ustād* sing, I think the *alāps* of Behāg, Mālkaus, and Darbārī Kāndra are the finest. On a still moonlit night, seated on one of the crowded housetops in the heart of Amritsar, to hear these songs without words, begun in the softest *pianissimo,* illustrated with the subtlest of gestures, accompanied only by the low burring sound of a *tambura,* this is an experience never to be forgotten! At such times our *ustād*—who could upon occasion shout with the loudest and hoarsest—proved himself a true artist, sensitive to every perfection both of sequence and quality of sound.

Gesture. A word may be said on gesture: those of Indian singers are of two kinds: the first, constituting a more or less conventional sign-language, is a kind of acting, accompanying song. This acting is developed to extraordinary perfection and expressiveness by such men as that supreme artist of Lucknow, Bindar Dīn; and much less often, by dancing-girls, and then more often in southern India than the north. Our *ustād's* gesture, however, belong to the second kind, where the hands are moved up and down or in complex wise following the music itself, an example of what has been called *empathy,* the transference of one own physical sensation into the *form* of a work of art. Not carried to excess, this form of unconscious musical gesture gives an additional expressiveness to song—suggesting and conveying a self-surrender to the rhythm and melody, which a wooden stillness would negative. In the two photographs of Abdul Rahīm given here, the first shows a quiet and peaceful gesture, as at the beginning of an *alāp,* the second (Pl. I, II) a more rapid movement accompanying a glide from a low to a high note, with wide separation of the hands. A second photograph on Plate II shows his pupil, Kali Khān, with a *tambura.*

Our *ustād* has never sung to any other accompaniment than a *tambura* and drums: he is one of an ever lessening number in India whose musical capacity

PLATE I

Abdul Rahīm, Kalānt, of Kapurthala

PLATE II

Abdul Rahīm, Kalānt

Kali Khān

Kāshmīrī Boys Singing

Krishna Boya Greb, Paṇḍit

Tirkno of Delhi

Abdulla Ḍār, Kāshmīrī Trouvère

has not been injured by reliance upon a harmonium. The notes of the *tambura* strings are: dominant, octave, tonic. These remain unchanged for all *rāgs.*

Voice production. The one point in which Indian singing is generally defective is in voice production; a point on which Ratan Devī has written as follows.[2]

The songs, or a large majority of them, need no criticism; they are masterpieces, but there is need of immediate improvement in the practical *use* of the voice.

Nearly all singers force their upper notes to a painful degree, though they appear quite unconscious of any undue effort and strain, and will go on singing the same passage repeatedly in exactly the same way, without any shame. This is usually followed by coughing and a clearing of the throat which they make no effort to conceal.

It is imperative that Indian singers be convinced that the *quality* of the voice is the vital part of it, and not the toneless volume of sound which they so delight in.

Deep breathing, a perfectly steady control of it, and absolute freedom of the throat are the primary essentials to beauty in singing; the power of becoming what is known as an accomplished singer follows these essentials, and depends mainly on the singers intellectual and artistic ability.

Not that Indian singers do not breath well; on the contrary, their breathing at times strikes one as something marvellous. They are able to sing passages of extraordinary length without any appreciable effort. But the same singer who can breathe so well, will in the following phrase, often quite short, take a breath several times in singing one word of perhaps only three notes' length.

One good singer of my acquaintance suffers from this fault, and in his case it is more than unfortunate because he has a voice of remarkable sweetness and roundness of tone—not big, though he makes the mistake of trying to make it so, and in consequence strains and shouts sometimes to such an extent that the result is a failure, and a most pitiful one. (It is utterly useless to expect to be able to use the throat and vocal chords as if they were made of cast iron.) To hear this man sing *pianissimo* passages of very intricate and subtle progression is wonderful, and an experience not to be forgotten, for at that time he is an inspired artist.

If only he, and many others like him, could realize that their power, the real power of carrying their audience outside time and space which is the treasured privilege of an artist, lies in the quality of the voice, and using that quality to its highest advantage by perfect freedom and entire absence of any strain or effort, India would probably possess singers such as no other country could boast of.

None can forecast the future of Indian music. At present it is rapidly vanishing before the gramophones, harmoniums and brass bands of modern Western commerce and modern Indian taste. Yet as it still exists, Indian music is the most significant of surviving Indian arts; if it dies, it will be of starvation rather than of inherent weakness. It has been, perhaps, the greatest aesthetic achievement of Indian civilization, the art in which that civilization has most perfectly expressed itself. Even now there are Indian musicians living of whom it is no exaggeration to say that they are quite supreme artists. Their music is the highest development of melody the world has seen—a science and an art comparable only with the whole achievement of Western music on different lines. In the course of another generation, this art may be finally lost; and once lost, it can never be recovered. It exists at present only in unwritten forms.

Not because it is Indian—though it be our one remaining treasure—but because it is great and splendid, because a thing of beauty is indeed a joy for ever, we who are moved by it, should somehow voice our enthusiasm. Such a motif inspires this little work: its authors, recognizing only too well its limitations, will be more than glad if it should be the means of introducing even one Western musician to a new world of art, still more if they might lead any Indian or English educationist in India to a knowledge of one of the many sides of Indian life ignored in every existing scheme of Indian education.

London ANANDA K. COOMARASWAMY
August 1912

NOTES

1. I have been given the explanation that the syllables so used are confined to those constituting the names of God: Ānantari, Nārāyana, Tarana.
2. *Modern Review*, October 1911.

6. Indian Music*

Music has been a cultivated art in India for at least three thousand years. The chant is an essential element of Vedic ritual and the references in later Vedic literature, the scriptures of Buddhism, and the Brahmanical epics show that it was already highly developed as a secular art in centuries preceding the beginning of the Christian era. Its zenith may perhaps be assigned to the Imperial age of the Guptas—from the fourth to the sixth century AD. This was the classic period of Sanskrit literature, culminating in the drama of Kalidasa; and to the same time is assigned the monumental treatise of Bharata on the theory of music and drama.

The art music of the present day is a direct descendant of these ancient schools, whose traditions have been handed down with comment and expansion in the guilds of the hereditary musicians. While the words of a song may have been composed at any date, the musical themes communicated orally from master to disciple are essentially ancient. As in other arts and in life, so here also India presents to us the wonderful spectacle of the still surviving consciousness of the ancient world, with a range of emotional experience rarely accessible to those who are preoccupied with the activities of overproduction, and intimidated by the economic insecurity of a social order based on competition.

The art music of India exists only under cultivated patronage, and in its own intimate environment. It corresponds to all that is most classical in the European tradition. It is the chamber music of an aristocratic society, where the patron retains musicians for his own entertainment and for the pleasure of the circle of his friends: or it is temple music, where the musician is the servant of God. The public concert is unknown, and the livelihood of the artist does not depend upon his ability and will to amuse the crowd. In other words, the musician is protected. Under these circumstances he is under no temptation to be anything but a musician; his education begins in infancy, and his art remains a vocation. The civilizations of Asia do not afford to the inefficient amateur those opportunities of self-expression which are so highly appreciated in Europe and America. The arts are nowhere taught as a social accomplishment; on the one hand there is the professional, proficient in a traditional art, and on the other the lay public. The musical cultivation of the public does not consist in 'everybody doing it', but in appreciation and reverence.

I have indeed heard the strange objection raised that to sing the music of India one must be an artist; and this objection seems to voice a typically

* A.K. Coomaraswamy, *The Dance of Shiva: Fourteen Indian Essays*, New York, 1924.

democratic disapproval of superiority. But it would be nearly as true to say that the listener must respond with an art of his own, and this would be entirely in accord with Indian theories of aesthetics. The musician in India finds a model audience—technically critical, but somewhat indifferent to voice production. The Indian audience listens rather to the song than to the singing of the song: those who are musical, perfect the rendering of the song by the force of their own imagination and emotion. Under these conditions the actual music is better heard than where the sensuous perfection of the voice is made a *sine qua non*: precisely as the best sculpture is primitive rather than suave, and we prefer conviction to prettiness—'It is like the outward poverty of God,[1] whereby His glory is nakedly revealed.' None the less the Indian singer's voice is sometimes of great intrinsic beauty, and sometimes used with sensitive intelligence as well as skill. It is not, however, the voice that makes the singer, as so often happens in Europe.

Since Indian music is not written, and cannot be learnt from books, except in theory, it will be understood that the only way for a foreigner to learn it must be to establish between himself and his Indian teachers that special relationship of disciple and master which belongs to Indian education in all its phases: he must enter into the inner spirit and must adopt many of the outer conventions of Indian life, and his study must continue until he can improvise the songs under Indian conditions and to the satisfaction of Indian professional listeners. He must possess not only the imagination of an artist, but also a vivid memory and an ear sensitive to microtonal inflections.

The thoery of scale is everywhere a generalization from the facts of song. The European art scale has been reduced to twelve fixed notes by merging nearly identical intervals such as D sharp and E flat, and it is also tempered to facilitate modulation and free change of key. In other words, the piano is out of tune by hypothesis. Only this compromise, necessitated in the development of harmony, has made possible the triumphs of modern orchestration. A purely melodic art, however, may be no less intensely cultivated, and retains the advantages of pure intonation and modal colouring.

Apart from the keyed instruments of modern Europe there scarcely exists an absolutely fixed scale: at any rate, in India the thing fixed is a group of intervals, and the precise vibration value of a note depends on its position in a progression, not on its relation to a tonic. The scale of twenty-two notes is simply the sum of all the notes used in all the songs—no musician sings a chromatic scale from C to C with twenty-two stopping places, for this would be a mere *tour de force.*

The 'quarter-tone' of *śruti* is the microtonal interval between two successive scale notes: but as the theme rarely employs two and never three scale notes in succession, the microtonal interval is not generally conspicuous except in ornament.

Every Indian song is said to be in a particular *rāga* or *rāginī*—*rāginī* being the feminine of *rāga*, and indicating an abridgement or modification of the main theme. The *rāga*, like the old Greek and the ecclesiastical mode, is a selection of five, six, or seven notes, distributed along the scale; but the *rāga* is more particularized than a mode, for it has certain characteristic progressions, and a chief note to which the singer constantly returns. None of the *rāgas* employs more than seven substantive notes, and there is no modulation: the strange tonality of the Indian song is due to the use of unfamiliar intervals, and not to the use of many successive notes with small divisions.

The *rāga* may be best defined as a melody-mould or the ground plan of a song. It is this ground plan which the master first of all communicates to the pupil; and to sing is to improvise upon the theme thus defined. The possible number of *rāgas* is very large, but the majority of systems recognize thirty-six, that is to say six *rāgas*, each with five *rāginīs*. The origin of the *rāgas* is various: some, like Pahārī, are derived from local folk song, others, like Jog, from the songs of wandering ascetics, and still others are the creation of great musicians by whose names they are known. More than sixty are mentioned in a Sanskrit-Tibetan vocabulary of the seventh century, with names such as 'With-a-voice-like-a-thunder-cloud', 'Like-the-god-Indra', and 'Delighting-the-heart'. Amongst the *rāga* names in modern use may be cited 'Spring', 'Evening beauty', 'Honey-flower', 'The swing', 'Intoxication'.

Psychologically the word *rāga*, meaning colouring or passion, suggests to Indian ears the idea of mood; that is to say that precisely as in ancient Greece, the musical mode has definite *ethos. It is not the purpose of the song to repeat the confusion of life, but to express and arouse particular passions of body and soul in man and nature.* Each *rāga* is associated with an hour of the day or night when it may be appropriately sung, and some are associated with particular seasons or have definite magic effects. Thus there is still believed the well-known story of a musician whose royal patron arbitrarily insisted on hearing a song in the Dīpak *rāga*, which creates fire: the musician obeyed under protest, but as the song proceeded, he burst into flames, which could not be extinguished even though he sprang into the waters of the Yamunā. It is just because of this element of magic, and the association of the *rāgas* with the rhythmic ritual of daily and seasonal life, that their clear outlines must not be blurred by modulation: and this is expressed, when the *rāgas* are personified as musical genii, by saying that 'to sing out of the *rāga*' is to break the limbs of these musical angels. A characteristic story is related of the prophet Nārada, when he was still but a learner. He thought that he had mastered the whole art of music; but the all-wise Viṣṇu, to curb his pride, revealed to him in the world of the gods, a spacious building where there lay men and women weeping over their broken arms and legs. They were the *rāgas* and *rāginīs*, and they said that a certain sage of the name of Nārada, ignorant of music and unskillful in performance, had sung them amiss, and therefore their features were distorted and their limbs broken, and until they were sung truly there would be no cure for them. Then Nārada was humbled, and kneeling before Viṣṇu prayed to be taught the art of music more perfectly: and in due course he became the great musician priest of the gods.

Indian music is a purley melodic art, devoid of any harmonized accompaniment other than a drone. In modern European art, the meaning of each note of the theme is mainly brought out by the notes of the chord which are heard with it; and even in unaccompanied melody, the musician hears an implied harmony. Unaccompanied folk song does not satisfy the concert-goer's ear; as pure melody it is the province only of the peasant and the specialist. This is partly because the folk-air played on the piano or written in staff notation is actually falsified; but much more because *under the conditions of European art, melody no longer exists in its own right, and music is a compromise between melodic freedom and harmonic necessity.* To hear the music of India as Indians hear it one must recover the sense of a pure intonation and must forget all implied harmonies. It is just like the effort which we have to make when for the first time, after being accustomed to modern art, we attempt to read the language of early Italian or Chinese painting, where there is expressed with equal economy of means all that intensity of experience which nowadays we are accustomed to understand only through a more involved technique.

Another feature of Indian song—and so also of the instrumental solo—is the elaborate grace. It is natural that in Europe, where many notes are heard simultaneously, grace should appear as an unnecessary elaboration, added to the note, rather than a structural factor. But in India the note and the microtonal grace compose a closer unity, for the grace fulfils just that function of adding light and shade which in harmonized music is attained by the varying degrees of assonance. The Indian song without grace would seem to Indian ears as bald as the European art song without the accompaniment which it presupposes.

Equally distinctive is the constant portamento, or rather, glissando. In India it is far more the interval than the note that is sung or played, and we recognize accordingly a continuity of sound: by contrast with this, the European song, which is vertically divided by the harmonic interest and the nature of the keyed instruments which are heard with the voice, seems to unaccustomed Indian ears to be 'full of holes'.

All the songs, except the *ālāps* are in strict rhythms. These are only difficult to follow at a first hearing because the Indian rhythms are founded, as in prosody, on contrasts of long and short duration, while European rhythms are based on stress, as in dance or marching. The Indian musician does not mark the beginning of the bar by accent. His fixed unit is a section, or group of bars which are not necessarily alike, while the European fixed unit is typically the bar, of which a varying number constitute a section. The European rhythm is counted in multiples of 2 or 3, the Indian in sums of 2 or 3. Some of the countings are very elaborate: Aṭa *tāla*, for example, is counted as 5 plus 5 plus 2 plus 2. The frequent use of cross rhythms also complicates the form. Indian music is modal in times as well as melody. For all these reasons it is difficult to grasp immediately the point at which a rhythm begins and ends, although this is quite easy for the Indian audience accustomed to quantitative poetic recitation. The best way to approach the Indian rhythm is to pay attention to the phrasing, and ignore pulsation.

The Indian art song is accompanied by drums, or by the instrument known as a *tambura*, or by both. The *tambura* is of the lute tribe, but without frets: the four very long strings are tuned to sound the dominant, the upper tonic twice, and the octave below, which are common to all *rāgas*: the pitch is adjusted to suit the singer's voice. The four strings are fitted with simple resonators—shreds of wool between the string and the bridge—which are the source of their 'life': and the strings are continuously sounded, making a pedal point background very rich in overtones, and against this dark ground of infinite potentiality the song stands out like an elaborate embroidery. The *tambura* must not be regarded as a solo instrument,[2] nor as an object of separate interest like the piano accompaniment of a modern song: its sound is rather the ambient in which the song lives and moves and has its being.

India has, besides the *tambura*, many solo instruments. By far the most important of these is the *vīṇā*.[3] This classic instrument, which ranks with the violin of Europe and the koto of Japan, and second only to the voice in sensitive response, differs chiefly from the *tambura* in having frets, the notes being made with the left hand and the strings plucked with the right. The delicate nuances of microtonal grace are obtained by deflection of the strings, whole passages being played in this manner solely by a lateral movement of the left hand, without a fresh plucking. While the only difficulty in playing the *tambura* is to maintain an even rhythm independently of the song, the *vīṇā* presents all the difficulties of technique that can be imagined, and it is said that at least twelve years are required to attain proficiency.

The Indian singer is a poet, and the poet a singer. The dominant subject matter of the songs is human or divine love in all its aspects, or the direct praise of God, and the words are always sincere and passionate. The more essentially the singer is a musician, however, the more the words are regarded merely as the vehicle of the music: in art song the words are always brief, voicing a mood rather than telling any story, and they are used to support the music with little regard to their own logic—precisely as the representative element in a modern painting merely serves as the basis for an organization of pure form or colour. In the musical form called *ālāp*—an improvization on the *rāga* theme, this preponderance of the music is carried so far that only meaningless syllables are used. The voice itself is a musical instrument, and the song is more than the words of the song. This form is especially favoured by the Indian virtuoso, who naturally feels a certain contempt for those whose first interest in the song is connected with the words. *The voice has thus a higher status than in Europe, for the music exists in its own right and not merely to illustrate the words. Rabindranath Tagore has written on this:*

When I was very young I heard the song, 'Who dressed you like a foreigner?', and that one line of the song painted such a strange picture in my mind that even now it is sounding in my memory. I once tried to compose a song myself under the spell of that line. As I hummed the tune, I wrote the first line of the song, 'I know thee, thou stranger', and if there were no tune to it, I cannot tell what meaning would be left in the song. But by the power of the spell of the tune the mysterious figure of that stranger was evoked in my mind. My heart began to say, 'There is a stranger going to and fro in this world of ours—her house is on the further shore of an ocean of mystery—sometimes she is to be seen in the autumn morning, sometimes in the flowery midnight—sometimes we receive an intimation of her in the depths of our heart—sometimes I hear her voice when I turn my ear to the sky'. The tune of my song led me to the very door of that stranger who ensnares the universe and appears in it, and I said:

Wandering over the world
I come to thy land:
I am a guest at thy door, thou stranger.

One day, many days afterwards, there was someone going along the road singing:

How does that unknown bird go to and away from the cage?
Could I but catch it, I would set the chain of my mind about its feet!

I saw that that folk song, too, said the very same thing! Sometimes the unknown bird comes to the closed cage and speaks a word of the limitless unknown—the mind would keep it forever, but cannot. What but the tune of a song could report the coming and going of that unknown bird? Because of this I always feel a hesitation in publishing a book of songs, for in such a book the main thing is left out.

This Indian music is essentially impersonal: it reflects an emotion and an experience which are deeper and wider and older than the emotion or wisdom of any single individual. Its sorrow is without tears, its joy without exultation and it is passionate without any loss of serenity. It is in the deepest sense of the words all-human. But when the Indian prophet speaks of inspiration, it is to say that the Vedas are eternal, and all that the poet achieves by his devotion is to hear or see: it is then Sarasvatī, the goddess of speech and learning, or Nārada, whose mission it is to disseminate occult knowledge in the sound of the strings of his *vīṇā*, or Kṛṣṇa, whose flute is forever calling us to leave the duties of the world and follow Him—it is these, rather than any human individual, who speak through the singer's voice, and are seen in the movements of the dancer.

Or we may say that this is an imitation of the music in heaven. The master musicians of India are always represented as the pupils of a god, or as visiting the heaven-world to learn there the music of the spheres—that is to say, their knowledge springs from a source far within the surface of the empirical activity of the waking consciousness. In this connection it is explained why it is that human art must be studied, and may not be identified with the imitation of our everyday behaviour[4]. When Śiva expounds the technique of the drama to Bharata—the famous author of the *Nāṭyaśāstra*—he declares that human art must be subject to law, because in man the inner and outer life are still in conflict. Man has not yet found Himself, but all his activity proceeds from a laborious working of the mind, and all his virtue is self-conscious. What we call our life is uncoördinated, and far from the harmony of art, which rises above good and evil. It is otherwise with the gods, whose every gesture immediately reflects the affections of the inner life. Art is an imitation of that perfect spontaneity—the identity of intuition and expression in those who are of the kingdom of heaven, which is within us. Thus it is that art is nearer to life than any fact can be; and *Mr. Yeats has reason when he says that Indian music, though its theory is elaborate and its technique so difficult, is not an art, but life itself.*

For it is the inner reality of things, rather than any transient or partial experience that the singer voices. 'Those who sing here', says Shankaracharya, 'sing God': and the *Viṣṇu Purāṇa* adds, 'All songs are a part of Him, who wears a form of sound.'[5] We could deduce from this a metaphysical interpretation of technique. In all art there are monumental and articulate elements, masculine and feminine factors which are unified in perfect form. We have here the sound of the *tambura* which is heard before the song, during the song, and continues after it: that is the timeless Absolute, which as it was in the beginning, is now and ever shall be. On the other hand there is the song itself which is the variety of Nature, emerging from its source and returning at the close of its cycle. The harmony of that undivided Ground with this intricate Pattern is the unity of Spirit and Matter. We see from this why this music could not be improved by harmonization, even if harmonization were possible without destroying the modal bases: for in breaking up the ground into an articulate accompaniment, we should merely create a second melody, another universe, competing with the freedom of the song itself, and we should destroy the peace on which it rests.

This would defeat the purpose of the singer. Here in this ego-conscious world we are subject to morality. But this morality is an illusion, and all its truths are relative: over against this world of change and separation there is a timeless and spaceless Peace which is the source and goal of all our being—'that noble Pearl', in the words of Behmen, 'which to the World appears Nothing, but to the Children of Wisdom is All Things'. Every religious teacher offers us those living waters. But the way is hard and long: we are called upon to leave houses and lands, fathers and mothers and wives to achieve an end which in our imperfect language we can only speak of as Non-existence. Many of us have great possessions, and the hardest of these to surrender are our own will and identity. What guarantee have we that the reward will be commensurate with the sacrifice?

Indian theory declares that in the ecstasies of love and art we already receive an intimation of that redemption. This is also the *katharsis* of the Greeks,[6] and it is found in the aesthetic of modern Europe when Goethe says

> *For beauty they have sought in every age*
> *He who perceives it is from himself set free—*

aus sich entrückt. We are assured by the experience of aesthetic contemplation that Paradise is a reality.

In other words the magical effects of a song in working mere miracles are far surpassed by its effects upon our inner being. The singer is still a magician, and the song is a ritual, a sacred ceremony, an ordeal which is designed to set at rest that wheel of the imagination and the senses which alone hinder us from contact with reality. But to achieve this ordeal the hearer must cooperate with the musician by the surrender of the will, and by drawing in his restless thought to a single point of concentration: this is not the time or place for curiosity or admiration. Our attitude towards an unknown art should be far from the sentimental or romantic, for it can bring us nothing that we have not already with us in our own hearts: the peace of the Abyss which underlies all art is one and the same, whether we find it in Europe or in Asia.

NOTES

1. Maheśvara, who wanders through the world a penniless and naked ascetic.
2. The *tambura* is a drone instrument with very rich overtones.—Ed.
3. Here the author seems to refer to the Tanjore *vīṇā*, its history going back to three hundred years or so.—Ed.
4. This is like the principle of 'conscious control' advanced by F.M. Alexander in *Man's Supreme Inheritance.*
5. Cf. the *Granth Sahib* (Japji xxvii): 'How many musicians, how many *rāgas* and *rāginīs* and how many singers sing Thee?'
6. Really speaking, the Indian theory of *rasa* cannot be equated with the Greek *catharsis* because the former embodies a much deeper and positive approach. —Ed.

II. ANTIQUITY OF *VĪṆĀ* AND ITS DESCRIPTION

7. The Parts of a *Vīṇā**

In Monier-Williams' Sanskrit dictionary, s.v. *vīṇā* we find description only of the modern instrument consisting of a low narrow sounding board with a gourd at either end (in the southern form there is only one gourd), seven strings, and nineteen frets. This type of *vīṇā*, in use at the present day, is also illustrated in numerous Rajput and Mughal paintings, and these take us back to the early seventeenth or late sixteenth century. Decidedly earlier than this is a representation in a fresco at Elūrā;[1] but this cannot possibly be of earlier than Rāṣṭrakūṭa date, and before this time it cannot point to any illustration of an instrument resembling the modern *vīṇā*. In any case, a *vīṇā* of the modern type, but simple form, is constantly represented, in Pāla sculptures, as held in the hands of Sarasvatī.[2] Possibly, too, the *anuttānālābu-vīṇā* of H., 145, a 'rounded-gourd' *vīṇā*, may have been of the later sort. On the other hand, we have a very large number of representation ranging backward from the late Gupta period to the beginning of the second century BC (Bhāja and Bharhut)[3] in which the *vīṇā* is consistently depicted as a kind of harp.[4] It is obviously with reference to this harp-*vīṇā* (German 'Bogenharfe') that this word as it occurs in classical Sanskrit and in Pali and early Prakrit literature is used. We may safely assume that the same harp-*vīṇā* is referred to in the still earlier Vedic literature; partly because of the a priori probability of a continuity of the tradition backward, partly because harps of various kinds actually existed in very early times (as recent discoveries at Ur have demonstrated), and also because the Āraṇyaka sources give us the same terms and imply the same forms as those later current. It is true that in some places various kinds of *vīṇā* are mentioned (cf. Keith, I, p. viii, note 2, and s.v. *tantra* below); but aside from this fact, the description and actual representations are so consistent and so much in agreement that we are justified in speaking of the harp-*vīṇā* here described as *the* old Indian *vīṇā*.

This old Indian *vīṇā* is a harp without a post; it has a hollow belly covered with a board or stretched leather; this belly is broader towards the back, where its end is rounded, and tapers toward the front, where it is continued into an upstanding curved arm, which often terminates in a little scroll like the head of a violin. The seven strings, one above the other, are stretched from this arm to the belly, forming as it were arcs to the crescent of the whole frame; they pass through holes in that flat surface (wooden or parchment sounding board) of the belly and must pass through and be fastened to its rounded under side. The weight of the instrument lies well back; it is held under the

* *Journal of the American Oriental Society*, Vol. 50, 1930.

Ill. 1

Ill. 2

Ill. 3

Ill. 4

Ill. 5

Ill. 6

The Old Indian *vīṇā* in use

left arm or in the lap, with its thin arm projecting forwards and upwards. From *Mayūrāṣṭaka*, I (M., p. 77) where the heroine is *baddhavīṇā*, 'girl with a *vīṇā*' it would appear that the *vīṇā* was, or at least might be, supported by a kind of sling (cf. s.v. *patta*, below), as apparently indicated in our plate, ill.2.

This old Indian *vīṇā* was used equally by men and women, either as a solo instrument (e.g. *Guttila Jātaka*), or as an accompaniment to song, as by Pañcaśikha on the well-known occasion of Indra's visit to the Buddha),[5] but even more often to accompany dancing (e.g. Div. 553, where queen Candraprabhā *nṛtyati*, and Aus. Erz., 31, where the queen *naccai*), whether dramatic or processional. In representations of dancing scenes it is not uncommon to find two *vīṇās* in use together ; sometimes also with an ensemble of flutes and drums, and (or) another stringed instrument, more like a European mandolin or Japanese *biwa*, described at the end of this article.

The old Indian *vīṇā* seems to have passed out of use altogether after the Gupta period; but the modern Burmese *sauṅ* which 'has a boat-shaped body of wood, with a skin stretched over it for a sounding board',[6] and thirteen silk strings, is very much like it.

The accompanying illustration is a restored representation of the old Indian *vīṇā*, based on numerous representations in the early reliefs (esp. Bharhut, Amarāvatī, Pawāyā).

II

The designations of the various parts of the old Indian *vīṇā* will now be dealt with in alphabetical order.[7]

Ambhaṇa (Skr.), the belly. Āit. Ār., III, 2, 5; ŚAr., VIII, 9 (compared to the belly of the human body). Evidently the boat-shaped, hollow body of the *vīṇā*; not merely the sounding board as rendered by Keith, 2. 254. Synonyms: *doṇī*, *doṇīkā* (Pali), Miln. 53. SN, IV, 197; *bhāṇḍa*, Manu, X, 49.

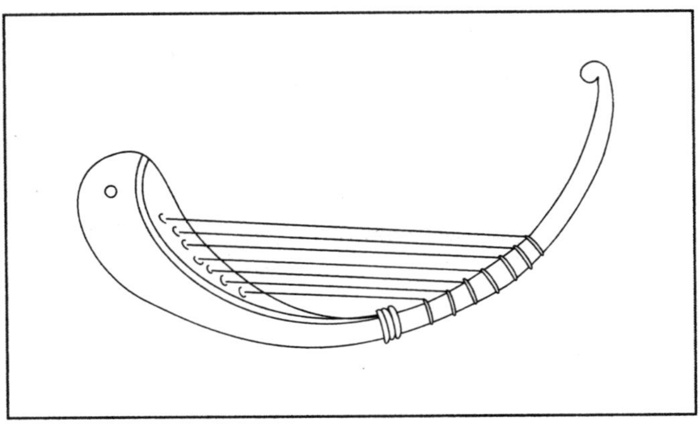

Fig. 1. The old Indian harp-*vīṇā*

Bhāṇḍa (Skr.), the hollow body of the harp, hence the harp itself. Manu, X, 49, *bhāṇḍa-vadana.* Synonym: *ambhaṇa, doṇī.*

Carma (Skr.), *camma* (Pali), leather, viz., the parchment sounding board. Āit. Ār., III, 2,5; ŚĀr., VIII, 9 ('with a hairy skin they used to cover *vīṇās*'). Miln. 53. SN, IV, 197. Cf. *godhā parivādentikā,* 'sounding lizard skin' (of a harp ?) , Jāt, VI , 580. Synonym: *pokkhara.*

Chidrāṇi (Skr.), *chiddāni* (Pali), holes. ŚĀr. VIII, 9. The holes in the sounding board, through which the strings pass. These holes, each ringed like an eyelet, can be clearly seen in a Bharhut pillar relief, unpublished, but in the Indian Museum, Calcutta; they are taken from this source in the restored sketch, Fig.1. In *Jātaka* No. 432 (Jāt. III. 507), a certain actor or dancer (*naṭa*) fastens his big harp (*mahāvīṇam*) about his neck and enters a river. The water enters the holes of the harp (*vīṇāchiddehi pāvisi*), and then its weight causes him to sink . In DhA., I, 215 a serpent is inserted through one of the holes (*chidda*) in the sounding board (*pokkhara*) of a *hatthikkanta-vīṇā,* in order that it may later emerge and bite the owner of the instrument (Story of Udena; for an Amarāvatī illustration, see *Rev. des Arts Asiatiques,* VI, pp. 101-2, and Pl. XXXII).

Daṇḍa (Skr.), *daṇḍa, daṇḍaka* (Pali), the arm of the *vīṇā,* forming with the *ambhaṇa* the whole frame.[8] *Mayūrāṣṭaka,* VII (M. p. 77), *vīṇīdaṇḍa* (*sic*) compared to a 'raised quivering arm';[9] SN,VI, 197; Miln. 53. In *Harṣacarita,* 252 (H., 223), *vīṇādaṇḍaḥ koṇābhighāteṣu,* a man is compared to the arm of a *vīṇā* by reason of the many cudgellings he has received. It would seem to be implied that not only the strings, but also the arm of the instrument might be intentionally struck with the plectrum (*koṇa, vādana*); this would produce a different kind of sound, and it would be possible in this way at least to emphasize the *tāla.* This possibility is supported by the *Guttila Jātaka* episode (Jāt., II, 253) where the competing players break successively all the strings of the *vīṇā,* and play finally on the arm alone (*suddhadaṇḍaka*). The arm of the *vīṇā* is proverbially bent (not 'broken' as rendered in Jāt., trans., II, 156) like a hunchback or an old man (Jāt., II. 225, *vīṇādaṇḍako viya saṁkuṭito*). Jāt., II, 226 resumes *saṁkuṭito . . . chinnatanti-vīṇā ' ti* which the Commentator interprets as 'bent like the body and arm (*sadoṇiko vīṇādaṇḍako*) if a *vīṇā* with broken strings'; and indeed, the curved shape of the whole frame would be still more conspicuous when the strings were broken.

The *Avadāna Śataka,* story 1 (Speyer, *Bibl. Buddh.,* III, 1902, I, 95, II, cited by Sachs) specifies Pañcaśikha's *vīṇā* as a *vaidūryadaṇḍa vīṇā*; in this case I hesitate to accept the meaning 'beryl' or 'lapis' for the material of the arm.[10] In Dh.A. 1. 433 the same *vīṇā* has its *daṇḍa* made of *veḷuva* (vilva) wood.

A synonym is *vaṁsa,* occurring in Aus. Erz., 56, and rightly identified with *daṇḍaka* by Meyer, *Hindu Tales,* 196. Here the *vaṁsa* is said to be *asuddha,* 'not clear', and this defect in the particular instrument is found to be due to the presence of a small stone in the *vaṁsa.*[11] Thus the arm of a *vīṇā* is hollow, and no doubt this hollow is continuous with that of the belly; perhaps, as the word *vaṁsa* itself suggests, the arm may sometimes have been made of bamboo. In any case the use of *vaṁsa* here goes far to explain ŚĀr., VIII, 9, where we have 'As this (human harp, i.e. body) has a *vaṁsa,* so that divine harp has a *daṇḍa*'; in other words, the human spine and the arm of the *vīṇā* are correlated, inasmuch as both are firm upstanding elements.

It will be observed that *śuddha* and *aśuddha* applied to *daṇḍa* as cited above are not corresponding terms; the *śuddha daṇḍa* is 'nothing but the arm of the *vīṇā*', the *aśuddha daṇḍa* is one that does not ring true.

Dhātu (Skr. and Pkt.), style of harp playing. There are four such styles, of which one, the *vyañjanadhātu* has ten variations (NS, 29, 52 and *Priyadarśikā,* III, 10).

Doṇī, doṇikā (Pali), the belly or body of the *vīṇā,* synonym of *ambhaṇa.* SN, IV, 197; Miln., 53; Jāt., II, 226 (*sadoṇiko vīṇādaṇḍako,* 'body and arm of the *vīṇā*', i.e. the whole frame.

Koṇa (Skr. and Pali), plectrum. H., §84, 'he taught the *vīṇā,* the plectrum firmly grasped in his hand'. Miln. 53 SN, IV, 197. Monier Williams cites *Rāmāyaṇa* II, 71, 26 and 81, which I have not consulted.

Synonym: *vādana.* In Keith 1, p. viii, *vādīnī,* H., p. 63, *koṇa* and *S.B.E.* XXXV, 84, *koṇa,* the terms are mistranslated 'bow', and Monier Williams s.v. *koṇa* has 'fiddle-stick' as well as 'quill of a lute'. Actually, no Indian *vīṇā,* whether ancient or modern, was ever played with a bow, nor for that matter is the European lute. The representations show that the plectrum with which the old Indian *vīṇā* was played had the form of a thin rectangular or pointed piece of wood, held between the thumb and forefinger. With such a plectrum, not only the strings but also the arm of the lute could have been struck, when necessary, with considerable vigour, and this elucidates *koṇābhighātesu,* cited above from H., § 252, s.v. *daṇḍa.*

The plectrum is very clearly shown in some of the illustrations on the Plate; also in Pañcaśikha's hand in a Gandhāran Visit of Indra, Foucher, *L'Art gréco-bouddhique du Gandhara,* I, fig. 247; where the player's hand is raised above his head as though he were striking with considerable force. But some reliefs seem to indicate a use of the fingers only without any plectrum.

Mūrcchanā (Skr.), *mucchanā* (Pali), pitch. SN, IV, 197 (with *bandhana,* possibly = *sādhāraṇa* of the NS). In Jāt., II, 249, Mūsila, *vīṇam uttamamucchanāya mucchetvā vādesi,* 'having tuned the *vīṇā* to a high pitch, played'; he then tunes the *vīṇā* lower to a medium pitch (*majjhimamucchanāya*), and finally plays with the strings slack (*sithile*). In *Mahāvagga,* V, 1, 16 we are told that if the strings of a *vīṇā* are too much or too little stretched, it is not in a fit condition to be played on.

Mucchanā is evidently used above (colloquially ?) in the older sense equivalent to *sthāna*, pitch or register, as in the older *Ṛkprātiśākhya* where also we have three registers, *uttama*, *madhya*, and *mandra* (cf. Caland et Henry, *L'Agniṣṭoma*, p. 462). *Sthāna* is used in this sense in the NS (XXVIII, 35), but now *mūrcchanā* has come to mean mode, and there are seven *mūrcchanās* in each register, of which (fourteen) seven are called *jātis*, a term practically equivalent to *rāga*. The NS (XXVIII, 25) illustrates these points by citing the tuning of two *vīṇās*, at first alike; the changes made by altering the pitch of the strings of one of them, and the comparison of the resulting notes with those of the other, show that a *vīṇā* could be so tuned as to take account of the twenty-two *śrutis*, in other words lent itself to all the niceties of musical theory and practise.

In the *Avadāna Śataka*, 17th story, it is expressly stated that Pañcaśikha playing on one string of a *vīṇā* produced the seven notes (*sapta svarāṇi*) and the twenty-one modes (*mūrcchanās*); it is hardly implied that there was anything miraculous about this, except in that the effects were obtained from a single string. *Mūrcchanā* is used here evidently in the later sense of 'mode', as in the NS. But the NS knows only fourteen *mūrcchanās*, seven for each *grāma*; perhaps the passage could be used to support the theory of the third *grāma*, not mentioned in the NS, but referred to by Śārṅgadeva in the thirteenth century as having 'retired to Indraloka'.[12]

The word *jātivīṇā* occurring in Jāt. II. 249, must I think mean, not as the translators have it 'a beautiful *vīṇā*', but one adapted to the playing of *jātis*. But whether it is to be deduced that not all *vīṇās* were so constructed as to make this possible, I cannot say.

It is evident from the above passages, and implied by many others in which the skill of the player is so emphasized and the effects of the music described as so moving, that the *vīṇā* could be tuned and kept in tune, and the same must be true of the modern Burmese *sauṅ*; the music cannot have been a mere drone. It is nevertheless very difficult to understand how such harps as this (which were also known to the Egyptians, Greeks, and Romans) could be tuned or kept in tune; not so much because no tuning devices are to be seen in the representations, as because it would be impossible to make an instrument with a curved frame and no post, were the frame even of steel, so rigid that a change of tension in one string would not alter that of all the others.

Patta (Pali), only in Miln., 53; rendered 'bridge of metal' in *S.B.E.* XXXV, 84, but apart from the fact that there is no authority for 'metal', the use of a bridge on the harp-*vīṇā* would be impossible, as the strings do not reach the sounding board side by side, but one above the other. I am inclined to think of 'sling' as a probable meaning as we know from *Mayūrāṣṭaka*, I, cited above, that the *vīṇā* was or could be supported in some such manner as by a sling.[13] This meaning also accords with the initial position of the word in the Miln. list of parts. A sling, passing over the right shoulder, seems to be represented in our Plate, ill. 2.

Pokkhara (Pali), the sounding board of a harp, made of stretched skin. It is pierced by the *chiddāni*, through which the strings pass, DhA., I, 215. Cf. *pokkhara* as skin of a drum. Synonym: *carma.*

Śiras (Skr.), head, i.e. the top of the arm (*daṇḍa*) of the *vīṇā.* In the representations the arm very often ends in a little scroll, which is evidently the 'head'. Āit. Ār., III, 2, 5; ŚĀr., VIII, 9.
Possible synonym: *upavīṇa.*

Sthāna (Skr.), register, high, middle, or low. See s.v. *mūrchanā;* and Caland et Henry, *L'Agniṣṭoma,* p. 462, with reference to *Sāmavidh. Br.,* I, 1, 8, 3.

Svara (Skr.), note. The seven *svaras* are produced by the seven strings (*Avadāna Śātaka,* 17th story; Caland et Henry, *L'Agniṣṭoma,* pp. 461, 462).

Tantra, tantrī (Skr.), *tanti* (Pali) strings. Āit. Ār., III, 2, 5; ŚĀr., VIII, 9; ŚSS., XVII; SN, IV, 197; Miln., 53; and *passim.* The strings are seven in number; one above the other, they pass through holes in the sounding board into the hollow of the body (*ambhaṇa*) and probably through its under side, there to be fastened as in the modern Burmese *sauṅ;* at this point on the under side of the belly the tuning devices must also have been placed. For the question of tuning see s.v. *mūrchanā.* Āit. Ār. and ŚĀr. have *tardmavatī,* apparently 'tightly strung'.
In. Jāt II. 253, the seven strings are broken in succession, the player performing on those remaining, and finally on the arm alone. The first string to be broken is called the *bhamaratanti,* 'bee-string'; as the first string to be broken would naturally be the top one, and as this being the longest would have the lowest note, we are able to identify the 'bee- string' as the top string. In the case of a harp for charming elephants (*hatthikkanta-vīṇā*) three of the strings have magical effects when struck (DhA., I, 215).
The *vīṇās* shown in the representations have sometimes seven, sometimes as many as ten strings.
The *vīṇā* with a hundred strings of ŚSS, XVII, XVIII, must have been a quite different instrument. I have seen in Kashmir an instrument resembling a Tyrolese zither, but with as many as a hundred strings, and played like a dulcimer.
Pace PTS *Pali Dictionary* s.v. *tantu,* this word in Jāt., V, 196, is the string of a toy, not of a musical instrument.
Stringed instruments generally, including the *vīṇā* in particular , are called *tantrikṛta* (NS, XXVIII, 9).
Synonym of *tantra: sūtra; Buddhacarita,* V, 55, (*suvarṇṇasūtrān*) 'golden strings', the instrument being here designated by the less usual term *parivādinī.*

Vād, Skr. root used of playing the *vīṇā,* e.g. Div. 553, *v° vādayati;* Jāt. II, 248, *v° vādesi;* Aus. Erz., 31, *v° vāei;* and *passim.* Instrumental music in general, as distinguished from song (*gīta*) and drama (*nāṭya*) is called *vādya* (NS, XXVIII, 7).

Vādaka (Skr. and Pali) *vāyaga* (Prakrit), (*vīṇā*), *vīṇā*-player. ŚĀr., VIII, 10; Jāt. II, 248; Aus. Erz., 56; and *passim.*

Vādana (Skr.), *vāyaṇaya* (Prakrit), the plectrum. Āit. Ār., III, 2, 5; ŚĀr., VIII, 9 (compared to the tongue of the human body, as a clapper, striker; ŚŚS, XVII, XVIII (*vādinī*). NS, XXVIII, 25. Aus. Erz., 31 (the *vāyaṇaya* slips from the players hand).

Synonym: *koṇa,* q. v.

Vīṇā (Skr. Pali, and Prakrit), in classical and earlier Sanskrit, etc., the harp-*vīṇā,* Bogenharfe. *Buddhacarita,* V.48, *rukmapatra-citrām . . . vīṇāṁ,* a *vīṇā* decorated with gold leaf. *Jātivīṇā,* Jāt. II, 248, see s.v. *mūrcchanā.* In the *Sakka-pañha Suttanta,* also in the *Dhammapada Atthakathā,* III, 226, Pañcaśikha's *vīṇā* is made of 'yellow *veḷuva* wood'; in the *Avadāna Śataka,* story 53, its *daṇḍa* is made of (or decorated with) *vaidūrya.* This *vīṇā* originally belonged to *Māra* (*veḷuva-daṇḍa-v°,* DhA., I, 433). The word *vīṇā* is, of course, of constant occurrence, and it would be superfluous to accumulate loci. According to Monier-Williams, the word *parivādinī,* which occurs in *Buddhacarita,* V, 55, where it is called big, and has golden strings, is a seven stringed lute (sc. harp-*vīṇā*); cf. *parivādentikā,* s.v. *carma. Hatthikanta-vīṇā,* for charming elephants, DhA., I, 215. *Anuttānālābu-vīṇā,* 'rounded gourd *vīṇā*', H., §145.

It may be added that many of the terms already listed occur not alone, but with the word *vīṇā* prefixed adjectivally, e.g. *vīṇā-daṇḍaka,* etc.

Vīṇā-āriā (Pkt. = Skr. *vīṇācārya*), an expert *vīṇā*-player, occurs in *Priyadarśikā,* III, 5.

III

The exact sense of some other terms is not so clear:

Aṅgulinigraha (Skr.), ŚĀr., VIII, 9 (compared to the joints of the human body), translated 'finger catches', Keith, 1, 55. Perhaps the bindings on the arm of the *vīṇā,* but the word order of the lists (see below) does not support this.

Śastravatī (Skr.) of ŚĀr. VIII, 9, is rendered 'sounding board' by Keith, 1, 55, but as the corresponding passage in Āir. Ār has *śabdavatī,* I am inclined to think that *śastravatī* is merely a predicate, 'gives out sound'.

Upastaraṇa (Skr.), ŚĀr, VIII, 9, rendered 'covers' by Keith, 1, 55. I cannot offer any suggestion.

Upavīṇa, upavena, perhaps the same as *śiras,* part beyond or added to the body of the *vīṇā.* Miln. 53, rendered 'neck' in *S.B.E.* XXXV, 84; but the position of the word in the Miln. list, immediately following *daṇḍa* (arm or neck), would seem to imply the meaning 'head' only; it is found also in the same position in SN, IV,197.

It should be observed that Skr. *upavīṇaya* means the playing of the *vīṇā* before someone, and not any part of the instrument itself (cf. *upanṛt*); it occurs in H. §82 in a charming passage where the bees are said to play with their feet a tiny (*bāla-*) *vīṇā,* the strings of which are the rosy rays of the royal earring (cf. 'bee-string', s.v. *tantra*).

In conclusion of this section, it will be worthwhile to cite the lists of terms as given in Miln. and SN., as they seem to be arranged in logical order, and this gives some clues to meaning. In Miln. 53, we have *patta, camma, doṇī, daṇḍa, upavīṇa, tantiyo, koṇa*: in SN., IV, 197, the same, omitting *patta.* In ŚĀr., VIII, 9, we have a reverse order; disregarding *śastravatī* which comes first, we have *śiras, daṇḍa, ambhaṇa, chidrāni, aṅgulinigrahās, tantrāni, vādana, carma.*

IV

ANOTHER INSTRUMENT

It remains to be observed that another stringed instrument, more like a lute or mandolin, also very like a Japanese *biwa,* is represented less often in the reliefs, either replacing the harp (e.g. Descent of the Bodhisattva, Amarāvatī, Indian Museum, Calcutta, reproduced in Burgess, *Buddhist Stupas of Amaravati and Jaggayyapeta,* fig. 7) or used together with it (our Plate, ill. 6, also in one of the Amarāvatī dancing scenes in the British Museum). This instrument has five strings, struck with a plectrum; and a corresponding number of tuning pegs at the top of the long neck (see accompanying restoration based on several representations). We do not know what this instrument was called; but as the other is best called a harp, so this is best referred to as a kind of mandolin. It seems to survive in the Travancore *dunduṇi* (Sachs, fig. 79), which is played with a plectrum, and has frets.

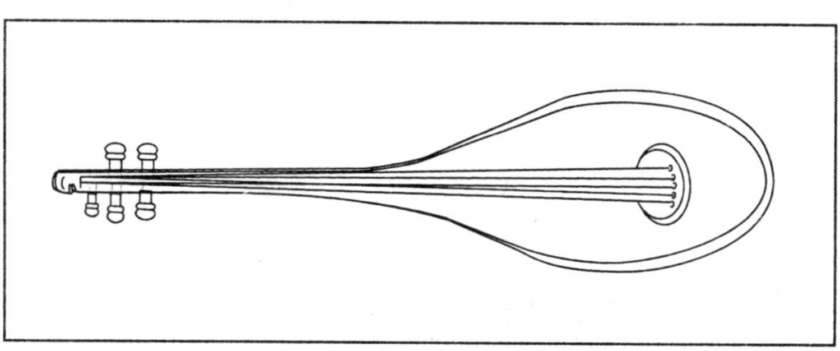

Fig. 2. The old Indian lute or mandolin.

LIST OF ILLUSTRATIONS ON THE PLATE[14]

1. Two seated female harpists, part of the chorus of a dance of apsarases, Bharhut, *ca.* 175 BC Indian Museum, Calcutta.
2. Harpist (possibly Pañcaśikha) walking, accompanying a processional dancer, Amarāvatī, *ca.* AD 200 British Museum.
3. One of two seated female harpists in a scene similar to fig.1, from a śuṅga railing pillar from Besnagar. Gwalior museum.
4. Two seated female harpists, part of the chorus in a dancing scene, railing medallion from Amarāvatī, *ca.* AD 200 British Museum.
5. Seated female harpist , part of the chorus in a dancing scene, from a pre-Kuṣāna architrave, now J 626 in the Lucknow Museum.
6. Dancing scene from an architrave, Pawāyā, Gwalior; Gupta. Harpist on right, 'mandolin' player on left.

NOTES

1. See *Ostasiatische Zeitschrift*, N.F. 3, 1926, p. 5 and fig. 3.
2. N.K. Bhattasali, *Iconography of the Buddhist and Brahmanical Images in the Dacca Museum*, pp. 181 ff. and Pl. LXIII.
3. Thus certainly three centuries older than suggested by Sachs, 139, and long before the time of the Periplus.
4. The latest representations of the old Indian harp-*vīṇā* I am able to cite is held by Sarasvatī, who is associated with Viṣṇu in a sculpture from Lakṣmaṇakāṭi, dateable about the eighth century AD (Bhattasali, loc. cit., p. 87 and Pl. XXXII.)
5. *Sakka-pañha Suttanta* (*Dīgha Nikāya*, II, 265); *Avadāna Śataka*, story 17.
6. Ferrars, *Burma*, 1900, p.176; Sachs, fig. 96 (after Scott O'Connor).
7. Abbreviations:
   Āit. Ār.: *Āitareya Āraṇyaka.*
   Aus. Erz.: Jacobi, *Ausgewählte Erzählungen in Māhārāshṭrī*, Leipzig, 1886 (=Devendra, *Uttarādhyayana Ṭīkā*).
   CT.: Cowell and Thomas, trans. of H., 1897.
   DhA.: *Dhammapada Atthakathā.*
   Div.: *Divyāvadāna*, edited by Cowell and Neill.
   H.: *Harṣacarita* of Bāṇa.
   Jāt.: *Jātaka*, edited by Fausböll.
   Keith,1: Keith, A.B., *Śañkhāyana Āraṇyaka*, 1908.
   Keith, 2: Keith, A.B., *Āitareya Āraṇyaka*,1909.
   M.: Quackenbos, *Sanskrit Poems of Mayūra*, 1917.
   Miln. : *Milindapañha* (Trenckner).
   NS: *Bhāratiya Nāṭya Śāstra.*
   Sachs: *Die Musikeninstrumente Indiens und Indonesiens*, Berlin, 1915.
   ŚAr.: *Śāñkhāyana Āraṇyaka.*
   SN: *Saṃyutta Nikāya* (ed. Feer, P.T.S.)
   ŚSS.: *Śāñkhāyana Śrauta Sūtra.*
   V.: *Vāsavadattā* of Subandhu, trans. By Gray, 1913.
8. Thus the rendering of *daṇḍa* alone as 'frame' in *S.B.E.*, XXXV, 84, is too comprehensive.
9. Cf. The use of *daṇḍa* in Subandhu, *Vāsavadattā*, 266-7 (V., pp. 127, 187); and the term *daṇḍahasta* used iconographically to designate the straight upper left arm of a Naṭarāja image.

10. Just as *vajra* is not always 'diamond', but very often 'adamantine', etc.
11. According to NS, XXVIII, 25, imperfections in sound (being out of tune, etc.) are attributed to defects either of the *daṇḍa,* or of the *vādana* (mistranslated 'resonance' by Grosset, *Contribution a Vétude de la musique hindoue,* p. 57) or of the strings. The *vīṇā* of Aus. Erz., 56, was at fault not only with respect to the *daṇḍa,* but also in having a hair on one of the strings.
12. For the *mūrcchanā* problems see Fox-Strangways A.H., *Music of Hindustan,* pp.106-12.
13. In Div. 553 , *hastād vīṇā śrastā bhūmāu nipatitā,* it is perhaps implied by *śrastā* that the sling is loosened, and therefore the *vīṇā* slips out of the player's hand.
14. For illustrations of Pañcaśikha with his *vīṇā* see my 'Early Indian Iconography 1, Indra', *Eastern Art,* Vol. 1, 1928. A Gandharan relief in which the plectrum is clearly shown is reproduced in *Mémoires concernant l'asie orientale,* III, 1919, Pl. IV, Fig. 5; but ib. Fig. 4 the *vīṇā* seems to be played with the thumb without any visible plectrum.

8. The Old Indian *Vīṇā**

When preparing my notes on the 'Parts of a vīṇā' (JAOS 50.244-253), I had not seen Canon Gilpin's learned discussion of Sumerian harps in *Music and Letters* for April 1929. In the course of this article it is pointed out that in 'nearly all oriental harps there is no front pillar', and that one of the Sumerian harps found by Mr. Woolley at Ur was a bow-shaped harp of this kind. 'This Sumerian harp had nails or pins on the arm which served as guides for the strings which were wound round them and the neck to the tension required'. The Burmese harp (*sauṅ*) has no such guides, but its tuning 'is dependent solely on hand tension or on the raising of the string on the sloping neck'. It is to be inferred that the old Indian harp *vīṇā* was similarly tuned by adjustment of the strings on the neck; and perhaps the word *aṅgulinigraha* should be understood as referring to pins on the neck similar to those of the old Sumerian harp.

Canon Gilpin then laments the current neglect of the comparative historical and ethnographical study of musical instruments and himself outlines the distribution of the bow-shaped and other kinds of harp. In discussing the Indian form he falls into numerous errors. 'The bow-shaped harp', he says, 'is not a musical instrument of India' (I am not quite sure what this is intended to mean); 'Hindustani music has no knowledge of it and it is stated that even Sanskrit treatises have no description of it' (but what else is referred to in the *Nāṭya Śāstra*?) 'if they had, it would probably be classed, like other foreign (!) instruments, as a *Vina*, which it certainly is not'.

Canon Gilpin is however aware that bow-shaped harps are represented at Sāñcī (where he antedates the reliefs by 150 years) and at Amaravati [*sic*] 'but here sculptures are not in the style and art of India', and mainly because Hsüan Tsang in the seventh century AD speaks of 'them' (actually, he did not visit Sāñcī, and it is not certain that he saw Amarāvatī) as 'ornamented with all the art of the palaces of Bactria', he calls the Indian bow-shaped harp 'the Bactrian harp' without more ado. Students of the history of musical instruments who are not Indianists should be warned against the adoption of this term.

In the first place, we know practically nothing about Bactrian art in the third century BC (as remarked by Rostovtzeff, 'we know so little of Bactrian art that it is mistake to explain *ignotum per ignotius*'), and certainly have no representations of bow-shaped harps which could be adduced as possible prototypes of the Indian forms: moreover, the Sāsānian harp, which presumably preserves an older Iranian type, is not bow-shaped but has a post. No evidence is brought forward for the implied view that the *vīṇā* constantly

* *Journal of the American Oriental Society*, Vol. 51, 1931.

referred to in Vedic, Sanskrit, and Pali literature is anything but the bow-shaped harp of the monuments. Again, the art of Bharhut, Sāñcī, and Amarāvatī is in fact essentially Indian—no one, for example, would suggest a foreign source for the architectural forms or the costumes, and it is a gratuitous complication to make a special case of the harp. What the reliefs show is not the imposition of a new culture on a clean slate, but simply a traditional culture pictorially recorded for the first time in permanent materials. Archaeological evidence, too, is every day establishing more and more clearly the continuity of pre-Maurya and post-Maurya civilization. The fact of Indo-Sumerian relationships established by the Sind valley excavations is quite familiar; and the occurrence of the bow-shaped harp in early Sumerian and surviving in Śuṅga Indian merely adds one more to the long list of cognate forms and types which equally in India and Mesopotamia derive from a common cultural source. Any theory of borrowing of particular forms at a later period has to be supported by individual and specific proofs. I therefore still maintain that the Indian bow-shaped harp is the *vīṇā* of the early literature, and see no reason to suppose that it was introduced into India precisely in the first quarter of the second century BC.

There is nothing mysterious about the presence of a bow-shaped harp in India. A more interesting and more difficult problem is presented by the fact that some time not long after the Gupta period a *vīṇā* of the modern type with a gourd or gourds replaced the earlier harp. What was the source of the modern form? Why was it preferred? How far do the Sanskrit treatises on music have in view the earlier, and how far the later kind of *vīṇā*?

It may be added that a very clear representation of a woman (*yakṣī*) playing the harp-*vīṇā* is reproduced on Pl. VI of T.N. Ramachandran, *Buddhist sculptures from a stupa nr. Goli Village, Guntur District*, Madras, 1929. Here the strings are struck by the fingers of the left hand only, without a plectrum. The rings on the neck of the *vīṇā* seem to indicate something more than a mere attachment of the strings, and perhaps some kind of tuning device is intended; at any rate, the forefinger is very definitely pressed down at one of the attachment points, as if to control the tone.

In Jātaka IV, 470, a girl plays on a *vīṇā* with her fingernails (*agganakhehi*) and sings, confirming the evidence of some of the reliefs, where no plectrum is shown.

I have received some valuable comments from Mr. J. Kunst, the well known scholar of Indonesian music, who has just been appointed to take charge of musical archaeological researches in Java. In this author's *Hindoe-javaansche Muziek-instrumenten*, 1927, p. 15, it is pointed out that the old Egyptian bow-harp was called *bjn. t.* or *bin*, which becomes *vini* in Koptic; and that the evident connection with Sanskrit *vīṇā* indicates either a common source (as would appear to me likely) or a later borrowing from Egypt (surely improbable inasmuch as the word *vīṇā* is already current in Vedic texts). Mr. Kunst here assumes also that as in Java, so also in India proper, the word *vīṇā* actually denoted a bow-harp. In either case, we have to do with a non-Aryan loan word in Sanskrit. For other data I quote Mr. Kunst's letter to me, dated 28 November 1930:

'The oldest illustration, I know, of the *modern* vina, you will find on one of the reliefs of the Bayon-temple of Angkor Thom, viz. on one of the interior galleries, East front, North wing (see Dufour, *Le Bayon d'Angkor Thom*, pl.120).

'The "mandolin"—better lute—you have found on the Amaravati-reliefs, appears, as you know, in many specimens and varieties at Barabudur. Further one specimen on the Shiva-temple at Prambanan (first basement, balustrade, South No. a), one in the hands of a bronze statuette of Sarasvati (Heine-Geldern, *Altjavanische Bronzen*, Tafel 14), and in those of two terracotta statuettes, found among the ruins of Madjapahit. (The latter two are slightly different and probably have undergone respectively younger North Chinese and Arabian influences.)

'The old Indian harp may have died in India proper rather early, but it has survived in Java, at least till the eleventh century. It occurs three times on Barabudur (resp. on relief Ia 1, Ia 52, and II 1), once on the Djalatunda-reliefs from AD 977, and once among the Ngandjoek-statuettes (in the hands of Sarasvati again, tenth century). On the continent it survived at least till the twelfth century, as it appears on the Angkor Thom relief, already mentioned.

'Today not only in Burma this small "boogharp" is to be found but also in Siam, where it is still called *p'hin*.

'The word *daṇḍa* occurs also in the old Javanese redaction (from AD 996) of the *Wiralaparwwa* (53), where it is combined with the word *pangupit* (something , that "pinches"?).

'The use of a plectrum is also shown on Barabudur—at least for the playing of the lute. See, for instance, reliefs O 102 and Ia 52.

'There are three different methods of tending and tuning the strings of those 'boogharpjes'. The first—and most primitive—is that of the harps from India proper, Turkestan. Further India and of two of the three Barabudur harps. It is done by means of chords.

'The second method is that by means of "plugs", wooden pins, to which the strings are fastened. This was the method of the old Egyptian and probably that of the other Barabudur, the Djalatunda, and the Ngandjock harps.

'Those plugs make it possible to count the number of strings. The Djalatunda-harp has four, the Ngandjock specimen seven (like the old Indian harps) and that of Barabudur ten strings.

'The third method, by means of real screws, is the most efficient. It is applied to some of the modern Negro harps (Uganda, Bakuba, Ubangi [Azandé, Mangbetu], Mandingo, Togo, Fan).

'The old Burmese lutes had three strings (see Courant, *Essai historique sur la musique des Chinois*, p. 177), so had most of the Barabudur lutes (for instance, reliefs O 125,II 1, and II 128), and the one of Prambanan. The rest of the Barabudur lutes have—seldom—two strings (reliefs O 102) or four strings (relief O 151). Instruments with five strings I do not know from Java.'

The accompanying reproduction of the Pawāyā dancing scene shows both the lute and the harp *vīṇā* very clearly.

Dancing scene showing the lute and harp vīṇā
From an architrave at Pawāyā, Gwalior
(Photograph by the Archaeological Dept. Gwalior state)

III. MISCELLANEOUS WRITINGS

9. Song-words of a Panjabi Singer*

If it sometimes happens that those who listen to Indian singers care more for the words than for the *rāgs* to which they are sung, they have this excuse, that the words are almost always beautiful, while the singer's voice is sometimes harsh or inexpressive.

The words of Indian songs are almost exclusively lyrical, never markedly dramatic. They are often deeply passionate; never sentimental like the modern drawing-room songs of Europe. They recall rather mediaeval English and Elizabethan hymns and lyrics. Their burden of love or sadness is expressed in many poignant similes. They contain allusions to every phase and moment of Indian life. They make frank and simple use of physical symbols to adumbrate the deepest spiritual experiences. A vein of mysticism runs through nearly all.

There is no marked distinction between art and folk songs. The same musician sings words that are written in purely country speech, as well as in several literary languages, though if he be a hereditary minstrel or court bard he will probably apologise for the former, and himself prefer high-sounding language and elaborate musical variations. As a musician indeed, rather than a poet, though he is usually both, he often cares most for *ālāp*, that is vocalization, or songs without words, and naturally looks down upon those who prefer any words to pure music. The words of many art songs however have a folk character, inasmuch as their composers' names are by no means always mentioned, and indeed usually unknown, and inasmuch as the words of these songs are orally transmitted and may be collected in varying versions. *It must always be impossible to draw any hard and fast line between folk and art songs, especially in a country like India, where the greatest works of literature have been for so long orally transmitted, and the musical notes of a song cannot be completely recorded and are rarely even partially written down.* The adoption of musical notation, and extended use of writing and printing for the song words will certainly effect future changes in the character of Indian music, and lead to a more marked divergence of character in folk and art music, as has been the case in Europe.

Broadly speaking we may say at present as regards words, those are of the folk whose motifs are naive, whose rhythm is well-marked, where repetitions and refrains are characteristic, the language simple, and the number of verses not very small. As regards music, the folk songs are often sung to quite definite tunes which are not classical *rāgs*. Their rhythm is emphasized. When sung to a *rāg*, this has a set form not admitting of *ad libitum* variation.

In art songs the language and motifs are more or less literary, the songs are short, often rather impressions or suggestions than of a descriptive character.

* A.K. Coomaraswamy, *Art and Swadeshi*, Ganesh & Co. Publishers, Madras, 1911.

The comparatively few words are sung with continual repetition to classical *rāgs* in forms admitting of almost unlimited variation. On the whole one may say that the art singer treats his words with less respect than the folk singer. In folk songs also words and tune are inseparable: the art singer will often sing any words to any *rāg*, occasionally sometimes quite unsuitable. An interesting feature in the songs of northern India, to which I mainly refer, is the way in which they illustrate the fusion or mixture of Hindu and Moslem elements in the existing culture. This is well seen in the song-words translated here, which are selected from the songs of an *ustad* of Kapurthala in the Panjab: they form only a fraction of his entire repertory.

A few words about this singer, in many respects a typical Panjabi musician of the present day, though on the whole much above the average, must be recorded before the actual songs are quoted. His name is Abdul Rahim, a hereditary 'Kalant', now a pensioner at Kapurthala. His father, Aliyas, was formerly employed at Jodhpur. Abdul Rahim has a profound knowledge of classical *rāgs*, and a sweet but not very strong voice, which he frequently overstrains, with expressive but often too violent gesticulation. His ancestors were Brahmans, forcibly converted in the time of Aurangzeb. Like so many other Panjabi Musulmans, the family retain many Hindu customs especially in connection with marriage, e.g. non-remarriage of widows. His faith in the Hindu gods is as strong as his belief in Islam. He is both devout, and also what is nowadays called superstitious. He would, for instance, hesitate or refuse to sing Dīpak *rāg*, unless in cold weather, for fear of creating actual flame. He is somewhat 'foresighted' and has prophetic dreams, and is like his father, something of a *fakīr*. Slight and delicate, gentle-mannered, patient, a first-rate teacher, an inveterate smoker of *hookah*, a great boaster, somewhat overfond of presents, learned in his own art, and at times truly inspired, yet finding that art now less appreciated than in the times of his predecessors—such are the salient characteristics of a rather pathetic figure, not without nobility, but such as the board school education of Indian universities finds little use for.

Turning now to the songs themselves, one finds that they belong to many languages—Panjabi (various dialects), Urdu, Hindi (various dialects, including Brij Bhāṣā), Sindi, Persian, Arabic. Those in Panjabi have naturally the most definite folk-character. This is most marked in the well known and delightful 'Lacchi', of which only a few verses are here translated. The air in this case is also purely folk and is not a *rāg*. Another and more poetical folk song is sung to Pahārī (mountain) *rāg* and has for its refrain 'They sell in the market'. A third, rather in Dogri than Panjabi, is sung to Jog ('separation') *rāg*. Perhaps the most beautiful, because of its perfection and directness is the three-line love song, sung to a very exquisite form of Pahārī, Chamba Pahārī. The windy freshness and, so to say, the solidity and noble gravity of the tune here rightly fit the passionate simplicity of the words. Like nearly all Indian love songs, it is a song of separation, a lament for loneliness. The references to Jammu and Kashmir perhaps need the explanation that the Kashmir court winters in Jammu and spends the summer in Srinagar.

'Death', a beautiful lament for the Beloved, expresses also the attachment of Panjabi people to their own land: in its third line, with pathetic hopelessness a woman prays her lord to return from the land of death, as if he had but gone away from home to another part of India or perhaps emigrated in search of work. Another little song, 'What means separation', is purely impressionist, telling even less of a story than the last, and is appropriately sung to one of the most beautiful of midnight *rāgs.*

In two songs reference is made to well-known romances. One is a Sufi quatrain, sung to Bihag or Malkaus in which reference is made to the Sindhi story of Punun and the other is taken from the Panjabi story of Hir and Ranjha. Hir tells her companions that by intensity of loving only, can union with the Beloved be attained: to forget love, even for a moment, is in itself separation.

The Panjabi *ghazal,* sung to Asa *rāg,* is again a song of separation or loneliness, with a Sufi interpretation: and the curious little song 'Only four days' seems to lament the shortness of life—too short for anything but play.

Of Hindu songs the first quoted likens true love to that of a tree that itself bears the heat but shades others and also by a subtle metaphor of the kite and the kite-flyer suggests that love itself may be the cause of separation between Lover and Beloved (in the perfection of Love these are one and there is no room for 'loving' and 'being loved'). The magnificent futility of the last couplet—as if Love could fail to bring with it pain, or as if to proclaim that none should love would deter any from loving!—would be hard to surpass. A second Urdu song, expresses the ecstatic indifference of the Sufi to the voice of any but the Beloved: its refrain *koi kuch bolo,* may be rendered '*aiunt, quid aiunt*' *aiant*!

A curious quatrain sung to Brindābanī Sāraṅg proclaims at once the singer's faith and mentions his favourite airs. It is a mixture of Musulman and Hindu ideas.

The invocation sung in Darbārī Kānaḍā, is an example of the prayers addressed to Moslem saints, usually asking for material blessings.

Passing now to the Hindi songs, we find many about Kṛṣṇa, sung by this Musulman with as much devotion as if he himself were a Vaiṣṇava. The first praises the one Lord appearing in many forms, proclaiming the unity of Brahmā, Śiva and Viṣṇu, though speaking most of the latter in His incarnations as Kṛṣṇa, Rāma and Narasiṁha. Three other songs are Gopīs' complaints, and refer to the boyhood of Kṛṣṇa at Brindāban.

One curious couplet asks 'What *yogī* is this?' Another complains 'You never speak to me now'. These are distinctly art songs, sung with constant repetition of words and phrases to complicated *rāgs.*

'How can I soften the heart of my Lover', literally *kapata ki gāṅṭh,* 'the knot in the heart', is again a lament for loneliness or separation: the phrase calls up the classic words of the *Muṇḍaka Upaniṣad.*

'Of him who sees that which is the highest and the lowest—*the knot of the heart* (*hṛdaya-granthiḥ*) *breaks*—all his doubts are solved—and his works become nothing.'

Thus in the words of Indian, as of Sufi songs, the human and divine are made one.

Much less beautiful than any of these, but yet characteristic, and much admired by minstrels, are the fulsome panegyrics sung to reigning kings by Court bards of the past. These are often sung to quite unsuitable *rāgs*—as if one should set words even more extravagant than those of 'See the conquering hero' to an air by Corelli or on the air of a mediaeval carol. In both the songs of praise quoted, the rulers hymned are hailed, with questionable taste and to modern ears, a suggestion of irreverence, as more than gods.

The few songs quoted from, as remarked, only a small part of one singer's repertory. If we except the two last, we cannot fail to admit their beauty and variety: and in India there are still thousands of singers possessed of a similar store. Would that some would collect, publish and translate some of these treasures! They will not always be at our disposal. For to the educated (as the victims of our Universities, Missionary and Nationalist colleges are by grim irony called) they are unknown and often meaningless. A well educated Indian professional man once asked me 'what is a Sufi?' On another occasion a well-known Nationalist enquired 'what is a Gopī?' Little use to think of an 'Indian people', when such are the fruits of 'Indian' education!

'LACCHI': FROM THE PANJABI*[1]

Aha, where Lacchi spills water,
Spills water, spills water, spills water,
There sandal grows—where Lacchi spills water.

Aha, Lacchi asks the girls
The girls, the girls, the girls,
Oh what coloured veil suits a fair complexion?

Aha, the girls said truly,
Said truly, said truly, said truly,
A veil that is black, becomes a fair complexion.

What then your fortune, Lacchi?
Your fortune Lacchi, your fortune Lacchi, your fortune Lacchi?
Lo ! Your boy like the moon, what then your fortune?

Who'll give you milk to drink Lacchi?
Drink Lacchi, drink Lacchi, drink Lacchi?
Your friendship with the goat-herds is sundered !
Who'll give you milk to drink?

*I have to thank my friend Dr. Paira Mall for assistance with most of these translations, especially those from the Panjabi.

'BĀZĀR VAKENDIAN'. RĀG PAHĀRĪ: FROM THE PANJABI[2]

Thou who knowest my inmost self, Beloved,
Who knowest myself,
They sell parched grain in the market—
If thou camest to my house, then would I tell thee my sorrow and joy,
My Beloved, who knowest my self.

Thou bowl of my dowry,
Thou bowl of my dowry
I sent thee away at midday, but now I wish I had not—
My Beloved, who knowest my self.

Thou veil of my dowry,
Veil of my dowry,
I earn but dishonour because of my friendship for thee,
My Beloved, who knowest my self.

On the high roof when I churn the butter,
When I churn the butter,
My parents rebuke me, thou alone can'st console—
My Beloved, who knowest my self.

They sell good spindles and fine in the market,
They sell in the market
The eyes of thee too are bewitching,
My Beloved, who knowest my self.

Aniseed they sell in the market,
Anissed they sell,
May Miranji cross-roads ever be populous, where first we had speech
My Beloved, who knowest my self.

They sell curds in the market,
Curds in the market,
Thou shalt sit near to wanton, lest they name thee a rake,
My Beloved, who knowest my self.

'RĀJĀ OF THE HILLS'. RĀG JOG: FROM THE DOGRI[3]

Come sometimes to our land, Oh Raja of the hills, come sometimes to our land !
God made your country prosperous, were I
A cloud, I would pour down on my beloved's land:
Come sometimes to our land!

'JASMINE'. RĀG CHAMBA PAHĀRĪ: FROM THE PANJABI[4]

Jasmine is blooming in my courtyard, and malthi gives scent near my bed:
O Beloved, thy service was in Jasmine but perforce must thou go to Kashmir
I send letters, but get not one in reply, to tell of thy welfare !

'DEATH'. FROM THE PANJABI[5]

My Lord has not spoken, he sulks since the afternoon—
The wheat crops are ripe, the rose trees in bloom—
I need not thy earnings, only come to the Panjab again!
You are setting out on your journey, but I am left desolate,
Ah, the house and the empty court do fill me with fear.

'THE HEART OF PUNŪṄ'. RĀG BIHĀG OR MĀLKAUS: FROM THE PANJABI[6]

There is separation's melting flame in the heart of Punūṇ, who daily lights its sacred fire:
The fire of disunion giveth no peace, as straw stays not its flame.
He himself is fire and fire-maker, he himself burns, and causes to burn.
How then can Hashm peacefully sleep, who has drunk of Love's cup?

'WHAT MEANS SEPARATION?' RĀG BIHĀG: FROM THE PANJABI[7]

I know not, dear one, how separation, from thee befell;
What is separation, he knows, who after meeting his parted,
I know not how it may be !

'PANJABI GHAZAL'. ASA RĀG[8]

Draw aside thy veil, O Beloved, that I may see thy face, who seek thy glance,
To see thy face for one moment I would sacrifice a hundred heads for thee!
All my comrades with their lovers lie on their beds,
I, luckless one, remain alone crying and crying and sighing.
Some come full, some go filled, the turn of some comes (and why not mine?)
Some desiring water swim in tanks, some called from their homes lie bosom to bosom:
I, luckless one, am nothing whatever if in the heart of my Lord I am forgotten.

'ONLY FOUR DAYS'. ASA RĀG: FROM THE PANJABI[9]

Only four days to play, Oh mother, only four to play!
To play and play!
Night has fallen, my Beloved is far from me, mother.
See, mother, thou woulds't have me spin—but four times

I bend the spindle,
Four, Oh mother, four only to play.

'HOW HĪR WON RĀNJHĀ?' FROM THE PANJABI[10]

The *sakhis* are asking thee, lovelorn Hīr, by what merit you won Rānjhā.
'I left my spinning, I left my carding, Love indwelt in each pore of my body—
By this merit, O *sakhis*, I won Rānjhā:
When my lovelorn soul onē moment forgot, that night Rānjhā came not.'

'RĀG MIAN KĪ BHAIRAVĪ'. FROM THE URDU[11]

They are fools who set their love on what does not seek for it:
No heart has the candle, in whose flame the moth burns to death.
Love thou in such wise as a tree—
Bearing the heat of the sun on its head and giving to others shade.
Beloved, think not that disunion from thee brings peace!
The wet forest wood smoulders day and night.
Beloved, in those days when thou wert the kite and I the string,
The wind of Love blowing made separation between us.
Beloved, had I known that Love would bring pain,
I must have proclaimed with beat of drum that none should love!

URDU GHAZAL* ASA RĀG[12]

I am mad for my Beloved:
They say, what say they?
Let them say what they will!
Take me for a fool or a mad man:
They say, what say they?
Let them say what they will!
I have nothing to do with them,
Whether they be pleased with me or angry,
May One only be gracious to me!
They say, what say they? Let them say what they will!

The Shaikh walks around his holystead;
I offer up myself at thy altar,
Call it shrine or hovel.
They say, what say they? Let them say what they will?
I have gazed on the glory and sheen of the cheeks of my Beloved,
I am burnt up as a moth in the flame,
I am as one drunken:
They say, what say they? Let them say what they will!

* See also *Essays in National Idealism*, Ch. XIII.

'MY FAITH AND MY RĀGS'. RĀG BRINDĀBANĪ SĀRAṄG: FROM THE URDU

Thou Allah! art all, who showed forth the model, so has knowledge come to the prophets:
My clan is Sayyid, my tribe is Moulah, my faith is in God and His prophet Muhammad.
My first is Bhairon, my second Mālkaus, my third Handol, my fourth Siri Rāg.
My fifth is Megh, my sixth is Dīpak, thus Sujān has sung.

'INVOCATION OF A SAINT'. RĀG DARBĀRĪ KĀNDRA: FROM URDU[13]

Hazrat Ghaunzal Samdani, Kutab of Rab, Oh Mir, come thou, who hast lordship over all sultans!
Friends of god, Abdulqadar Jailani, make easy what is hard, give us bodily health, thou hast Allah's favour on thee!

'PRAISE OF THE LORD'. RĀG NEKI KĀNDRA: FROM THE HINDI[14]

Thou as Kṛṣṇa appearedst, as Rāma, Lakṣmaṇa without stain Thyself took form!
Thyself, Mahādeva, art a shining beam, Thyself art Brahmā who established the Vedas,
Thyself the three Vedas, Thyself the three worlds, Thyself the *tapas*, Thyself the *yogī* who Yoga established,
Thyself became fish of the sea, Thyself took the form of Narasiṁha!

'GOPĪS' COMPLAINT'. RĀG BIHĀG: FROM THE HINDI[15]

See, *sakhīs,* how Kṛṣṇa stands!
How can I go to fetch water, my mother-in-law?
When I go to draw, water from Jamuna!
There meets me the young boy of Nanda!

'GOPĪS' COMPLAINT'. RĀG MĀLKAUS: FROM THE HINDI[16]

When I go down to draw water, O mother, at Yamuna *ghāṭ*
He catches me by the clothes and twists my hand:
When I go to sell milk,
At every step Gokula seeks to stop me.
When he is so obstinate what can I say?

He ever comes and goes: why does this Youngling so?
He takes hold of my arm and shuts my mouth, and clasps me close:
I will make my complaint to Kaṅsa Rājā, then I shall have no fear of thee!

'WHAT YOGĪ?' RĀG BIHĀG: FROM THE HINDI[17]

What *yogī* is this, who wanders about with rings in his ears and ashes smeared?
Some perform meditation, some dwell in the woods, some call on thy name with devotion!

'YOU DO NOT SPEAK TO ME'. RĀG DARBĀRĪ KĀNAḌĀ: FROM THE HINDI[18]

You say nothing to me, though Phāgan has come
Every watch you are sulky with me, always I see you with others.

'HOW CAN I SOFTEN THE HEART OF MY LOVER?' RĀG LACĀRĪ: FROM THE HINDI[19]

How can I loosen the knot that binds the heart of my beloved?
All my *sakhīs* well-decked have gone to their lovers,
But I sit alone eating poison.

PRAISE OF RĀJĀ RĀM OF GWALIOR: FROM THE HINDI

Rājā Rām, Rājā of Rājās, Mahārāj, Adhirāj, accomplished, Treasury of ten kinds of knowledge!
Whosoever asks his wish is heard and reward obtained: do homage to Him who established the Vedas, Rājā Rām!
Eight *siddhis*, nine *nidhis* dost thou bestow,
And gifts to the wisdom-endowed!
Tānsen gives praise. He who worships the Lord will freedom win, may Rājā Rām live through four ages!

(by Tān Sen)

PRAISE OF RĀJĀ RĀM OF JODHPUR. RĀG BHOPĀLĪ: FROM THE HINDI[20]

Sun of India! Rasa Rāja! at the splendour of whose might even Rāma trembles,
The seven islands, nine spheres, and four continents have done homage to thee, the powers of the air take refuge in thee,
O glory of the Lunar dynasty, they praise thee in fear, thou the ruler of Jodhpur!

(by Fakir Aliyas, father of Abdul Rahim)

NOTES

1. Ratan Devi and A.K. Coomaraswamy, *Thirty Songs from the Panjab and Kashmir*, ed. Prem Lata Sharma, IGNCA, New Delhi, 1994, p. 23.
2. Ibid., p. 14.
3. Ibid., p. 76.
4. Ibid., p. 15.
5. Ibid., p. 24.
6. Ibid., p. 26.
7. Ibid., p. 25.
8. Ibid., p. 24.
9. Ibid., p. 23.
10. Ibid., p. 25.
11. Ibid., p. 26.
12. Ibid., p. 27.
13. Ibid.
14. Ibid., p. 21.
15. Ibid., p. 11.
16. Ibid., p. 9.
17. Ibid., p. 12.
18. Ibid., p. 19.
19. Ibid., p. 22.
20. Ibid., p. 8.

10. Indian Music*

BOOK OF WORDS

1. PRAYER. RĀGIṆĪ BHAIRAVĪ

Jo tu racho samāna deyā tāre nainoṅ pargāsh:
Tohe nā basārūṅ dvāra, dvāra tore gāye gāye.
Tero nāma Naraṇkar, kahi na jāve, aprāpar,
Sura nara muni kara bichāra.

Thou Who didst make the world, glory shines in Thy eyes:
May I never forget Thee for ever and ever, and ever sing Thy praise.
Thy name is Narankar, which cannot be told of, ineffable,
Albeit Gods and men and sages have pondered thereon.

2. PRAYER. RĀGA IMAN-KALYĀN

Sumarana karungī maiṅ torā tu sāhaba merā,
Mere guna auguna tujhe hī zāhr,
Tu karīm, tu rahīm, tero hī nāma sattāra.

O Thou, my Lord, I will remember Thee,
My virtue and my lack are known to Thee,
Thou the Merciful, Thou the Compassionate, Whose Name is Forbearance.

3. PRAYER. RĀGIṆĪ NEKI KĀNHṚĀ[1]

Āpe āye Krishna banābana, Rāma lakshmaṇa niūṅ kalaṇka,
Āpe Mahādeva jotī sarūp, āpe Brahmā jina veda rachāye,
Āpe tina, āpe tarloka, āpe jatī satī, ape jogī jina joga rachāye,
Āpe banāye macch kacch sāgar, āpe Narsingh rūpa sadaye!

As Kṛṣṇa Thou didst appear, and as Rāma and Lakshmaṇa void of stain,
Mahādeva art Thou, in the likeness of light, and Brahmā art Thou revealing the Vedas!
Thyself the three, the Triple Cosmos, Thyself adept, essential, Thyself the Yogī who Yoga established,
Thyself wast the fish, the Tortoise, the sea, and Thine the form of Narasiṃha!

* Publication details of this writing could not be traced.

4. HINDI LOVE-SONG. RĀGIṆĪ DARBĀRĪ KĀNHRĀ[2]

Aba tuma bolata nahīn, muse āyo phāgan māsa:
Pahara pahara para rusata muse, jaba dekhūṅ un pāsa.

You never speak to me now, though Spring has come:
You are wrath with me each hour, and always I see you with those others!

5. HINDI LOVE-SONG. RĀGIṆĪ LACHĀRĪ[3]

Kauna jatana kara kholūṅ, mere piya ke man meṅ kapaṭa[4] *kī gāṇṭha?*
Kauna jatana kara kholūṅ?
Saba sakhiāṅa mila bana ṭhana nikasīṅ,[5] *maīṅ beṭhī bisa gholūṅ!*

How shall I loose the knot of anger that binds the heart of my Beloved?
How loosen the knot?
Each of my comrades lies in her lover's arms, but I sit alone eating poison!

6. HINDI LOVE-SONG. RĀGIṆĪ BIHĀG[6]

Piyā bicharana horī maiṅ jānat nahīn:
Bicharana ki gat so kau jānī jo mil bicharī—
Horī maiṅ jānat nahīṅ!

I know not, Beloved, how separation from thee befell:
She knows what separation may be, who has met and parted—
I know not how it befell!

7. MILKMAID'S COMPLAINT OF KṚṢṆA. RĀGA MĀLKAUS[7]

Jala bharana calī, rī māī, Jamanā ghāṭa,
Añcara pakaṛa mora[8] *maṛorata hātha:*
Hauṅ jo jāta Gokula dudha becena,
Bāta ghāta muse karatārā.

Aiso langar dhīṭvar, morā kyā kahūṅ?
Bāra bāra āvata jāvata, ye to kāhe ko karata ye nauhāra?
Bhūja pakaṛata, morā mukha mundata kara, pakaṛata mohe girhūṅ lagāve;
Jā pukāṛūṅ Rājā Kaṅs ke āge, na ḍara mānūngī torā!

Whenever I go to fill my pitchers at Jamunā bank, O Mother,
He pulls my veil and grips my wrist:
When I go to Gokula selling milk,
He intervenes in my affairs.

And so perverse he is, what shall I say?
He ever comes and goes, why does this youngling so?
He takes me by the arm and shuts my mouth, and clasps me close;
I will complain before King Kaṅs, then I shall have no fear of thee!

8. MILKMAID'S COMPLAINT OF KṚṢṆA. HINDI, RĀGIṆĪ BIHĀG[9]

Dekho sakhī ghanayā roke ṭhāḍaro ghaila!
Pānī bharane kaise jāūṅ, morī ālī?
Hūṅ jo calī jamanā jala bharane,
Āge milgayo nanda ke chaila!

Behold, my dear, how Kṛṣṇa stands and hinders me!
How can I go to fetch my water, my dear?
Whenever I go to the Jamunā for water
There stands before me Nanda's ne'er-do-well!

9. MILKMAID'S COMPLAINT OF KṚṢṆA. HINDI, RĀGIṆĪ ASĀVARĪ[10]

Maiṅ rahiyāṅ so birahana ke pāsa, paṛa paṭa būnda chamaka bhīganāra!
Bāta ghāta mohe rokata ṭokata, kauna jāne piya hamāre ghāta
Bayiāṅ se pakaṛa-kara karana bāta, nita uṭha leta bahuta ūbhe sāsa!

I delayed by that lovesick lad, the rain-drops pattered down, and all was soaking wet!
He interferes with all my doings, naught avails in my affair my dear.
He takes me by the arm, and talks away, and ever heaves great sighs!

10. THE YOGĪ. PANJABI, RĀGIṆĪ BIHĀG[11]

Kauna jogī havāṅ, kānan mundrāṅ,
Bhasam bhabhūta, lagāvān rumāvāṅ?
Eka japa tap karan, eka banbāsa meṅ,
Eka tero nāma dhyāvan ripāvāṅ.

What *yogī* is this, with rings in his ears and ashes smeared, who wanders about?
One tells his beads, one dwells in the woods, another calls on Thy name with devotion!

11. PANJABI LOVE-SONG. RĀGIṆĪ PAHĀRĪ[12]

Mere hāla deyā mehrmāṅ, ve ḍhola, bazāra vakendiāṅ ve holāṅ—
Ghar āveṅ ta dukha sukha pholāṅ, mere dukhandiāṅ jamna, ve ḍhola.

Mere dāja deyā ve kaṭoriā, tenūṅ sikhr dopehre toria,
Tor pacchtaniāṅ, ve ḍhola, mere hāla deyā mehrmāṅ, ve ḍhola.

Mere dāja deyā ve dopaṭiā, yārī lake kujh na khaṭia,
Kuṛī badnāmī ve ḍhola, mere hāla deyā mehrmāṅ ve ḍhola.

Ūchi mārī te dudh pai riṛkāṅ, menūṅ sāre tabar diyāṅ jhiṛkāṅ,
Terā ve dalāsa, ve ḍhola, mere hāla deyā mehrmāṅ, ve ḍhola.

O thou who knowest my inner being, Beloved! They sell parched pulse in the market-place—
Wouldst come to my house, I would open to thee my weal and my woe.

Thou bowl of my dowry, I sent thee away at noon,
But now I repent, my Beloved, who knowest my inner being!

Thou veil of my dowry, because of my friendship for thee, I nothing earn
But a girl's disgrace, Beloved, who knowest my inner being, Beloved!

High on the roof when I churn the milk, elders reproach me,
Thou alone canst console, my Beloved, who knowest my inner being!

12. DOGRI LOVE-SONG. RĀGIṆĪ CHAMBĀ PAHĀṚĪ[13]

Angan phūlī chamba mālatī, khaṭ nālue chhoṛī bāsa—
Jamūāṅ dī karnī pyāriā chākrī, Kāshmīrāṅ dī pai mahīm.
Chiṭṭhiāṅ bhejdā, koi nahīṅ āondā terā sukha sānd!

Jasmine blooms in my courtyard and wafts its scent across my bed—
O Beloved, thy service was in Jammū, but it is to Kāshmīr thou must go.
I send thee letters, but none come back to tell of thy welfare!

13. ḌOGRI LOVE-SONG. RĀGIṆĪ JOG

Kadī āṅvanāṅ māṅde des, ve pahāraṅ vāliā rājiā:
Barsāṅ mahbūbāṅ vale des, badli hovāṅ vārive jhaṛ kar devāṅ!

Some day come to my country, O Rājā of the hills!
I would be like the dripping rain upon the land of my Beloved;
were I a little cloud I would have sheltered thee, Beloved!

14. BANDE MĀTARAM. RĀGA SHĀHĀNĀ

SANSKRIT WORDS BY BANKIMCHANDRA CHAṬṬOPĀDHYĀYA

Bande Mātaram! sujalām suphalām malayaja-śītalām,
Sasya śyāmalām mātaram, Bande Mātaram!

Śubhrajyotsnā-pulakita-yāminīm,
Phulla-kusumita druma-dala śobhinīm,
Suhāsinīm sumadhura-bhāṣiṇī sukhadām varadām mātaram, Bande Mātaram!

Trimśat-koṭi kaṇṭha kalakala nināda karāle,
Dvitrimśat-koṭi bhujayīr-dhṛta karakara vāle,
Kathayanti janāsthvām katham mātara-balām,
Bāhu-baladhāriṇīm ripu-dala vārinīm,
Namāmi tāriṇīm mātaram, Bande Mātaram!
Tvameva vidyā tvameva dharma tvameva marma tvamhī prāṇā śarīre,
Tvaiva pratimā māta dṛshyate prati-mandire:
Tvamhī Durgā daśa-praharaṇa dhāriṇī namāmitvām,
Amalām atulām subhalām sukhadām sasya-śyāmalām mātaram, Bande Mātaram!

My Motherland I sing—her splendid streams, her glorious trees,
The zephyr from the far-off Vindhyan heights, her fields of waving corn,
The rapt'rous radiance of her moonlit nights, the trees on flower that flame afar,
The smiling days that sweetly vocal are—the happy, blessed Motherland.

Her will by seventy million throats extolled, her power twice seventy million arms uphold,
Her strength let no man scorn!
Thou art my head, thou art my heart, my life and soul art thou,
My soul, my worship, and my art: before thy feet I bow.

As Durgā, scourge of all thy foes, as Lakshmī, bowered in the flower
That in the water grows: as Bānī, wisdom, power, the source of all our might,
Our every temple doth thy form enfold, unequalled, tender, happy, pure.
Of splendid streams, of glorious trees, my Motherland I sing,
The stainless charms that e'er endure; the verdant banks and wholesome breeze
That with her praises ring.

15. PERSIAN SUFI ODE OF SHAMS-I-TABRĪZ[14]
KASHMIRI FOLK-AIR[15]

Chi tadbir ay Musalmānān? ki man khūdrā namīdānam;
Na tarsā wa yahudīyam na gabram nai musalmānam.
Na sharqīyam na gharbīyam na barrīyam na bahrīyam . . .
Na az mulk-i-Irāqīyam, na az khāk-i-khurasanam.

What is to be done, O Muslims? for I know not myself.
I am neither Christian nor Jew, nor Gabr, nor Muslim,
I am not of the East, not the West, nor of land nor sea . . .
I am not of the kingdom of Iraq, nor the land of Khurasan!

16. KASHMIRI SUFI ODE BY ABDULLA ḌAR[16]

Yāra itam lāgavo yārānatai,
Zoqa chus nālānatai shoqa cāne, &c.

Come hither, Beloved, join friendship with me,
For thy love my heart is lamenting!

17. KASHMIRI *REVERDIE*

Hosh karta latiye, toshtar osh hai āv!
Hī vathrāvtai ḍabidālānas, hī-hindi chi rozān nāv.

Awake, my friend, rejoice, the Spring has come!
Spread jasmine on the balconies, the name of jasmine long endures.

18. KASHMIRI LULLABIES

Dŏd ceto dāma dāma, gali gale, ho ho karayo adakale.

Drop by drop drink milk, little by little.
Oho! I will rock thee, lisping one.

Lālo lŏli manz ālare, gūr ho karai kanadūr garai, lālo.

In my lap I'll lay thee, lullaby, my child;
I'll rock thee and make thee ear-rings!

19. KASHMIRI LULLABY, BY MAHMŪD GĀMĪ WOMEN'S DANCE AIR

Guri guri karayo, kanake dūro, &c.

I'll rock thee, my ear-ring, my ear-ring!

NOTES

1. See Ratan Devī and A.K. Coomaraswamy, *Thirty Songs from the Panjab and Kashmir*, ed. Prem Lata Sharma, IGNCA, New Delhi, 1994, p. 20 (though the text is the same, the translations are absolutely different).
2. Ibid., p. 19 (the translations vary).
3. Ibid., pp. 21-2 (the translations vary).
4. *Kapaṭa* literally means 'deceit'.
5. *Bana ṭhana nikasiṅ* literally means 'going out well-dressed and adorned'.
6. Ibid., p. 25 (the translations vary).
7. Ibid., p. 9 (the translations vary).
8. *Āñcara pakaṛa* means 'he pulls the loose end of my sārī'.

9. Ibid., p. 11 (the translations vary).
10. Ibid., pp. 16-17 (the translations are not similar).
11. Ibid., p. 12 (the translations vary).
12. Ibid., p. 14 (the song is longer in the *Thirty Songs* . . . and the text and the translation differs).
13. Ibid., p. 15.
14. For the complete ode, with translation, see R.A. Nicholson, *The Dīvān of shams-i-tabrīz*, pp. 124-7.
15. Ibid., p. 64 (the translation is different and the ode is longer).
16. Items 16-19 are found in their complete versions with different translations in the *Thirty Songs from the Panjab and Kashmir.*

11. Introduction to *The Study of Indian Music**

The time is perhaps far distant when it will be possible to write a connected history of Indian music, tracing its origins, development, and old age. It is clear, however, that its golden age—that period so short in the history of any art cycle, and so prepotent in determining the modes of both art and life for long subsequent periods—must lie far back from the present. Not improbably, that golden age coincided with the moment of greatest achievements in drama, Kalidasa, and for the theory, Bharata. Long anterior to this, however, music was a most highly cultivated—perhaps the most highly cultivated—of Indian arts, and to the present day it has remained the most continuously vital and most universally appreciated art of India. Taking together what has been lost, and what remains, music is, then, the most complete expression of the soul or genius of the Indians—a mirror faithfully reflecting their inner life. That English orientalists and educationists have so long ignored this music, is the measure of their misunderstanding of India.

While it is true that, until modern times, music has remained in the best sense one of the most popular of Indian arts, it is also true, though with exceptions, that it has been neglected and despised, for example, by Aurangzeb, as well as by more modern puritans. But the music remained too intimately associated with religion, with the drama, and with life, whether courtly or popular, and was too faithfully guarded by the traditions of the guilds for it to be possible that it should die out altogether. There are to be found even now, for the most part at the courts of Indian *rājās*, or in specially musical towns like Lucknow, Tanjore, and Poona, a few *ustāds* who are artists of high, and even of supreme rank; but they belong to an order that is passing away.

The neglect of centuries, as in so many analogous cases, has proved less disastrous than the renewed patronage of a few decades. The constant use of the tempered harmonium; the endeavour to adapt Indian modes to the purposes of tenth or fifteenth-rate brass bands maintained by Indian *rājās*; the absence of any aesthetic element in modern Indian education; the mania for English accomplishments: all these causes have actively contributed to the degeneration of Indian music. By degeneration, I mean literally confusion, a running together, and destruction of bounding-lines; a process quite distinct from any natural waning of vitality at the latter end of an art cycle.

Now that life has changed, so that the old music, however splendid, no longer expresses race-intention (we are no longer united by such an intention), there are two considerations that must weigh with us, when we think of Indian music; to maintain the memory of our past experience, as an

* Foreword by Anand K. Coomaraswamy, in the *Introduction to The Study of Indian Music*, by E. Clements, London, 1913.

interpretation and inspiration and delight, and to clear the way for new creators. For both these ends it is necessary to escape from the confusion into which the theoretical part of Indian music has unfortunately fallen. It is here, I think, that Mr. Deval has done great service in applying a purely experimental method to the analysis of the actual intonation of thoroughly trustworthy hereditary musicians. Mr. Deval's work, the results of which are published in his 'Hindu Musical Scale and the Twenty-two Srutees', deserves the highest praise. It is true that Mr. Deval did not succeed in his endeavour to improve his case by importing aid and corroboration from scientific acoustics and Sanskrit philology; but I think that certain of his critics fall into more serious error when they judge the results of his patient and invaluable experimental work by weakness or inaccuracies in his method of presentation.

The preparation of the *śruti* harmonium, and the presentation of the general results of Mr. Deval's work, combined with a critical discussion of the theory of music according to Bharata and Śāraṅgadeva in Mr. Clements' most interesting book, mark, I think, an epoch in the scientific study of Indian music. It will at any rate be possible for future writers, even when they disagree with Mr. Clements, to say more clearly and definitely than heretofore, what they exactly mean; and still more important, for future recorders to make a nearer approach to a true transcription of the Indian *rāgas*. I cannot but hope that Mr. Clements will himself extend his studies in this direction. It may be a long time before we have as full and as exact a knowledge of Indian music as we have of Indian literature; but if that time ever comes, it will, I am sure, be acknowledged that the work of Mr. Deval and Mr. Clements did much to clear the way for such a development of knowledge.

I should like to say a word of warning with regard to the *śruti* harmonium. This instrument is to be welcomed, in any case, as infinitely preferable, from the standpoint of intonation, to the tempered harmonium now in common use. It is a valuable tool, and may be used for purposes of research, and also for class teaching, where the instruction of large classes (a process foreign to the Indian conception of educational method) is unavoidable. Thus used, the *śruti* harmonium will serve the ends of exact knowledge, and will not (as the tempered harmonium now does) destroy the sensitiveness of the Indian ear to those 'hair's-breadth' distinctions which are essential to a highly evolved art of pure melody. *But, as I think, no harmonium of any kind should ever be regarded as a substitute for the tambūrā, because the quality of tone of the tambūrā is so infinitely superior to that of the harmonium, to say nothing of other aesthetic and social considerations; above all, the harmonium should never be used as an accompaniment to the voice, leading or imitating note by note.* This last, even with the *vīṇā*, would be foolish; with a blatant instrument like the harmonium, incapable, moreover, of any gliding from note to note, it becomes repulsive.

Much the same argument applies to the use of a system of notation; for the purposes of exact knowledge—most desirable as a means of escape from the present chaos—it is very important that a suitable method of transcription should be discovered. *But the publication of Indian music in staff notation, without warning that the scale is other than that usually implied by that notation, tends to the destruction of the character of that music in the same way as the use of a tempered harmonium.* It is for the purposes of science, of teaching, of the preservation of existing songs, and the making of these accessible to Western students, that a notation is now so necessary—above all, for the preservation of what is so rapidly disappearing, and must soon be lost. But if it be possible to maintain still, amidst the general popularization of music in the modern and democratic sense, a tradition of master-musicians in pupillary succession, as heretofore, then for these it is far better that the method of oral transmission should be maintained. No matter if the masters in different parts of India do not all agree; the very divergences of their *rāgas* may be an expression of local character. *But it is not for the sake of variety that I would preserve the system of oral transmission; but rather because this is the true method of learning for an artist, because every singer so taught must be in some degree a composer (he is taught, not merely to repeat a given song, but to sing in a given mode and mood), and because it is so great an advantage for the true musician to need no external aid to memory, such as a printed score.* Indeed, I suppose that even if we succeed in recording the greater part of Indian music as it still survives, the music itself cannot persist as a part of everyday life unless it is thus handed on as a sacred tradition.

In any case it is much that the existing music should be recorded and analyzed for the student of whatever time or country. The necessity of such a record in India need not be dwelt upon; but perhaps the most valuable result of the growing interest in Indian music would be realized if the time ever comes when, in the words of Captain Day, 'the study of the national music of the country will occupy, as it should, a foremost place in all Indian schools', and certainly, also, in the Universities. But I should also like to emphasize the importance of this study for Western musicians; not only as a means of better understanding the heart of India, but also because it must be in the long run disadvantageous to ignore one half of the world's experience in any art. If Indian music is very different from Euorpean—and the fundamental difference is less than at first sight appears—then all the more reason for the Western musician to enlarge his outlook. Perhaps even, in the words of M. Bourgault-Ducoudray, Oriental music may 'provide Western musicians with fresh resources of expression, and with colours hitherto unknown to the palate of the musician'. At least we may feel certain that both for us, and for the Western student, the exact study of the science of Indian music is a necessary process in the interests of progress and interpretation.

It is then with gratitude that I have accepted Mr. Clements' invitation to write a preface to his learned and stimulating work; in so doing I wish to specially commend both the whole subject of Indian music, and this book, to the notice of all Indians and Englishmen who have any voice in determining modes of education in India.

ANANDA K. COOMARASWAMY

London,
12 September 1912

12. Rāgamālā Poems*

Each of the thirty-six *rāgas* and *rāginīs*, or modes of Indian music has its own peculiar emotional content or burden, and its own associations: a Rāgamālā is a 'garland' of poems describing the various situations and circumstances corresponding to the burden of each mode. There exist no printed editions of these poems, but they are often found inscribed upon the pictures which illustrate at once the poems and the music. The situations in question are the various conditions of love in union and love in separation, or happy and unhappy love, as experienced by the different classes of heroes and heroines known to Indian rhetoricians. The poems appear to be contemporary with the earliest picture series, and so of the late sixteenth or early seventeenth centuries: their authors are almost unknown, but many of the poems deserve to stand beside the words of the most famous Hindi poets.

The theme of the poems and the burden of the music, as we have said, is love. This is, indeed, par excellence, *the* theme of classical Hindi poetry. *All this literature has been created in an environment saturated with the stories of spiritual devotion symbolized in terms of human love—an environment in which a divorce of physical and spiritual experience could hardly have been imagined.* In the Rāgamālā poems, however, the love that is spoken of is a definitely human experience: and while in Vidyāpati and other Vaiṣṇava writers we find the spiritual experience related in human terms, here we find the terms of spiritual experience used to describe a human passion. Thus, in a poem for Vibhāsa Rāginī we find:

> '*Her body burns with furnace heat, like a devotee (tapī), most intently centred (samādhi dhari dhīra), on the thought of the beloved,*
> '*Sunk in the trance (dhyāna magna) of considering the loved one.*'

Again, in Gandhārī Rāginī

> '*Like a vairāgī (ascetic who has renounced the world) she makes a prayer (japa-tapa) of her beloved's name,*'

that is to say, she makes her beloved her God, telling his name as a nun repeats the name of God on her rosary.

The rainy season is especially the time for the enjoyment of love, for it is

* *The New Orient*, New York, 1924, pp. 76-8.

then that the lord returns from his military expeditions to pass the wet season at home and with his lady: and an auspicious season, for without the rain-laden clouds the crops must fail. And so, in another version of Vibhāsa Rāginī we find:

'Heavy black clouds are gathering auspiciously,
flashes of lightning illumine the sky,
Her body blossoms like a flower for the meeting
with her darling, she stands entranced.
Enthralled by the thought of her lord's embrace,
there is bliss in her heart.'

Again, in Meghamalāra Rāginī:

'Now breaks the storm with unutterable fury, the
lightning flashes and brings down the rain,
In this glad hour and season of passion, lord and
lady play together.'

With their dual inheritance of classical Sanskrit love-lore and of folk-experience, these poems reveal a profound acquaintance with love, characteristic of Hindu culture. It is from knowledge born in him, far more than from any peculiar or personal experience that the poet speaks, and his audience is constitutionally qualified to understand his every allusion. Very often in phrases of startling poignancy and in the simplest and most direct way, the most vivid images may be evoked—we realize that we too, 'nous avons passé par là'.

'When all the ritual of the god of love has been
done, the morning dawns, and it groweth cool,
Now is Vibhāsa wearied out, and sweet sleep steals
upon the bed.'

Expecting her lord's return, the loving bride may be waiting in the garden, where

'There are flowers beyond telling, the more one
looks the more the heart is charmed,
Flowers upon flower in their fragrance, marvelous vision.' (Gaurī Rāginī)

Or, she may be

'So drowned in the trance of meditation upon the
beloved that she seems like a carven image.' (Guṇakalī Rāginī)

When her lord returns,

'Though her heart is deeply moved, and her eyes
are smiling, she utters not a word,

And most demurely turns away her face.' (Bairārī Rāginī)

She may have cause for jealously, if her lord,

> *'Wantonly dallies with another sweetheart, on a*
> *gaily coloured bed in the palace.'* (Bhairava Rāga)

And then she sits,

> *'With hanging head and silent lips compressed: a*
> *great tide surges through her as she remembers love,*
> *Stretching her limbs in sorrow, a rain of tears*
> *pours from her eyes, like a broken chain of*
> *pearls.'* (Paṭamañjarī Rāginī)

Very often, however, he is as devoted as she: even in battle,

> *'There is deep love in the heart of the beloved.'* (Naṭa Rāga)

If her lord becomes an ascetic she too renounces the world,

> *'Ashes on her limbs, a deer skin about her waist,*
> *deep sunken in sorrow, with dishevelled hair,*
> *Delighting not in jewels nor any pleasure, taking*
> *only food according to rule.'* (Setamalāra Rāginī)

We might extend indefinitely our extracts from this special branch of Hindi poetry: but enough has been said to reveal at once its profound charm, and its significance as the picture of an inner life whose intimations are so generally veiled for us by the unfamiliar forms of a manner of life that is not our own.

13. The Bee-song of Sūr Dās*

The poet Sūr Dās, *c.* 1483-1563, is very generally regarded as the greatest of the 'Eight Seals', all poets of the middle or late sixteenth century,[1] so designated because their works are regarded as the classical standards of the variety of western Hindi known as Braj Bhāṣā, the tongue of Braj, that is to say of the country round Brindābana, the scene of the *Bāla Līlā* or Enfances of Kṛṣṇa.

'Sūr Dās excelled in many styles of composition. A large number of episodes and passages from the *Bhāgavat Purāṇa* were reproduced by him in exquisite verse, and he was the writer of a great number of lyrics in connection with the worship of Kṛṣṇa and Rādhā, which were collected together in the *Sūra Sāgara* and the *Sūrāvalī*. . . . Altogether he is credited with having composed as many as 75,000 verses. Sūr Dās holds a very high place in literature. Some Indian authorities would give him the foremost place amongst Hindi poets, though most persons would reserve that honour for Tulasī Dās. An oft-quoted couplet referring to Hindi poetry says, 'Sūr is the sun, Tulasī the moon, Kedav Dās is a cluster of stars, but the poets of today are like so many glow-worms giving light here and there.'[2]

The Bee-song (*Bhramara-gīta*) is one of the two famous songs so named, which are included in the *Sūra Sāgara*. For those who are at all familiar with the *Kṛṣṇa Līlā* and its general significance, the song will require little explanation. It may be remarked, however, that in Vaiṣṇava mysticism human love is regarded as the image and outward form of spiritual experience. Thus, the milkmaids of Brindābana, amongst whom Kṛṣṇa was brought up as the foster-son of father Nanda and of Yaśodā, are all of them lovers of Kṛṣṇa, and He is their Beloved; for His sake they disregard all attachment to worldly honour, surrendering themselves to him in utter self-forgetfulness. At last, He must leave them to play His part in world: He overcomes Kaṅsa of Mathurā, and becomes a king in Dvārikā. Without Him the milkmaids are desolate. Then, He sends his friend Udho, who is very clever, wise and bold, to comfort Nanda, Yaśodā and the milkmaids; not by any promise of return under the old conditions, but by so instructing them that they may realize Him not in the phenomenal guise of son or lover, but as ever present in the heart, ever accessible in the depth of one's own being. In other words, He will teach them Yoga and Vedānta, in place of personal devotion (*Bhakti*); and He writes a letter which Udho is to read aloud. Udho goes then to convert the milkmaids to the path of knowledge.

* *The New Orient*, Vol. III, No. 2, July 1926, pp. 51-4.

N.B. The used text contains corrections in the author's hand after publication.

But he finds them hard to convince; their experience has been a reality to them, and they will not exchange it for the worship of a 'painted figure on a wall'. Udho is overcome by the arguments, and himself acknowledges that the path of Love is superior to the path of knowledge. It is easy to see that the poet himself is on the side of Love; and in fact he uses the occasion to outline the two Ways, and to exhibit the victory of Love. When Udho returns to Kṛṣṇa, all the pride of his knowledge has left him, he has himself become as one of the milkmaids, a *Bhakta.* Kṛṣṇa responds to him, at the same time humorously congratulating him on the success of his mission.

All the ideas to be found in a poem of this kind are the common property of a whole school of devotional theology, and of mystical poets; scarcely anyone but rests upon a more secure foundation than that of individual fancy or inspiration. In consequence, the perfection of the poet as such can hardly be revealed in a translation; profound and beautiful thoughts are voiced by mediocre and by the greatest poets alike, the only difference is one of skill or art. To appreciate these differences it is necessary to study the original. In spite of this, I believe that the readers of *The New Orient* will be glad to read in a literal translation an example of the work of this master of Hindi verse.

It remains only to add that amongst the many names by which Kṛṣṇa is known, he is spoken of in the poem also as Gopāla (The Herdsman) and Lord of Govardhana, Śyāma (The Dark), Hari (Glaucous),[3] Braja's Darling, the Lord of the Yadus. The translation follows:

Hear and lend ear, how Udho taught, as Śyāma required of him, the Doctrine of the Unconditioned:

Milkmaids: 'Someone is coming on the road where Kṛṣṇa went away—a flute is sounding sweetly, as though 'twere Braja's Darling Himself!'

Then they all ran up in crowd, and there they found Udho; they brought him to Nanda's[4] house, and could not contain their hearts for joy,

They offered him holy water and the service of lights and the brow-spot, and using a whisk of grass they sprinkled his head with curd, they set before him full golden jars, and circumambulated him.

The yard became a very mass of milkmaids, and all sat down together, and setting before him full jars of water, asked after his health.

And the health of Vasudeva and Devakī, and even of Kubja, and how did Akrūra and the lovely Balarāma?

And all of them clasping his feet, enquired if all were well with the Herdsman: then Udho was drowned in love at the sight of the Braja folk.

And he thought in his heart that perhaps the Herdsman had been wrong to forget the love of Braja, and to wish to instruct its folk in Yoga—

'All their body, like the moth, is afire with love, while Hari is like the flame of the lamp, and void of all love for them.'

Then Udho took out the letter that Kṛṣṇa had written, but he could not read a word, so full was his heart.

He could not make out the lines, because his eyes were filled with tears: at the sight of the milkmaids' love the pride of his knowledge fled away.

Then this way and that he turned, and wiped the tears from his eyes, and resolving to set forth the tale for the milkmaids' weal, he turned again—

'That end for which the Sages strive, and man not attain, *that* way is shown by the milkmaids of Braja, who cast off the snare of the world.'[5]

Listening to Udho, they sat with downcast eyes, as though they had asked for nectar and been given the burning venom of a snake—

'We are helpless girls, how can *we* understand the path of Yoga, how can we abandon our devotion to Kṛṣṇa, to worship a figure painted on a wall?'

'He is not to be reached nor grasped, without bound, fundamental, Uncreate, Whom all men worship, the ultimate Unattached;

Brahmā abides in your eyes and the tip of your nose (so near He is), Indestructible, Undecaying, His glory shines without effort.'

'But, Udho, if he has no eyes, nor nose, nor mouth, how could he have stolen and eaten curd? If he has no feet, why did they bind him to the mortar?'

Whom did we rock in our arms, who prattled and lisped?[6] This is the ruling, Udho, of one who has no eyes indeed!

It would seem the ever-shifting Illusion has destroyed the two eyes of such a man, and opened the 'everlasting eyes of wisdom' to see most strange things!

Now why not summon the 'Uncreate', *he* will explain the mystery 'without beginning or end, nor born of a father and mother'!

'Tis like a man who has filled his house with cattle-dung, and wonders where to tie his cattle: let him look at home, why should one show him another muck-heap?

It is stupid of Kṛṣṇa to try to teach us Yoga: he says we have gone astray— but have *we* gone astray, or perhaps some other folk (who need not be named)?

Love arises from Love, and by Love the way is found; the whole world is bound up in Love, by love one reaches the ultimate goal.

True Love is the dispensary of Liberation-in-This-Life, nought else but Love; by True Love, indeed, by *this* one finds Gopāla.

Come now, Udho, honestly speak the truth, whether the sweet Way of Love is gold or glass?

'On whatsoever your faith is firm, hold to *that* Rule':[7] tell us, O Honey-bee, which is the better, Yoga or Love'

At the sound of the milkmaids' words, Udho forgot his Rule, and wandered through the forests, singing the Herdsman's praises, (his body) like an open flower:

Now he fell at the milkmaids' feet, exclaiming. '*Yours* is the hallowed Rule!', now he ran to embrace the trees, overcome by love:

'Blest are the milkmaids, blest the Herdsman, blest the forest-wandering cows, blest the Holy Land where Kṛṣṇa walked,—

I came to teach, but I am taught,' and Udho returned to the Lord of the Yadus, wearing a milkmaid's guise:

He did not remember the name of the Lord of the Yadus, but called him Master Herdsman, he prayed Him to go to Braja to show Himself once at least to the milkmaids—

'Have you forgotten the joys of Brindābana, that you are living here?', and deeming Him Lord of Govardhana (who now was in sooth the Lord of the Yadus), Udho clasped His feet.

'Come, now, Udho, tell me all the Rule of Love in Braja'—but his eyes were filled with tears, and he could not speak a word.

Sūr Dās says that even Śyāma's wits wandered, and wiping away the tears with His yellow scarf, He said 'You certainly preached the path of Yoga well!'

NOTES

1. '*Aṣṭachāpa*' is the collective epithet for the eight poets commissioned by Śrī Vallabhācārya to compose songs in Braj-bhāṣā, depicting *Kṛṣṇa-Līlā*. '*Chāpa*' in this compound stands for the composer's signature.—Ed.
2. F.E., Keay, Hindi Literature.
3. *Hari* literally means He who 'steals' or enamours.—Ed.
4. Kṛṣṇa's foster-father, corresponding to Joseph in the Christian gospels.
5. This is what Udho is thinking, while nevertheless he reads the letter that so much annoys the milkmaids.
6. The allusions are to the *Bāla-Līlā* (enfances): the milkmaids assert that Udho cannot explain away the mischievous baby they loved.
7. Perhaps an allusion to *Bhagavad Gītā*.

14. Toḍī Rāginī*

Anonymous†

Most! marvellously wrought of God, fairest
 in all three Worlds, without exception, is Toḍī;
With hands of nectar redolent, she stands in a grove,
 memories of love innumerably uprising in her heart.
At the sound of her lute they forget their quarrel,
 and stand at gaze in utmost beauty.
Nearby there is a lily lake of limpid waters like the
 Ganges' wave;
She stretches out her hands to the fallow deer, and
 with her hands she calls them to her side.
She is under the spell of the Beloved, her eyes are
 shining, the Beloved in her heart, and has left the world:
Beguiling the hearts of the deer, this Toḍī stands in
 the grove.

* *The New Orient*, May/June 1924, Vol. II, No. 1, p. 36.

†Literally translated from the Hindi text of British Museum MS. Or. 2821.

15. Music in India, Indian Music, Indian Musical Instruments*

MUSIC IN INDIA

Apart from the folk music (lullabies and songs of labour, etc.) and from processional and wedding music, the music of India is either devotional or chamber music. The devotional music includes on the one hand that of the ancient Saman chant, which has probably come down essentially unchanged during three millenniums, and on the other an infinite variety of hymns addressed to the Deity under various names. Chaitanya, in the fifteenth century, in effecting a revival of Vaiṣṇava faith by his impassioned hymns, was only repeating the methods of the Buddhist Ashvaghosa 1400 years earlier. In the South the great collection of Śaiva hymns known as the *Tevāram*, and the songs of Mānikka Vācagar, are sung in temples, and those who hear these songs are moved to tears. Art music remains almost entirely in the hands of an hereditary profession, consisting of *ustads*, or 'masters' (of whom the most famous was Tān Sen in the sixteenth century), and of dancing girls. These are maintained by aristocratic patrons or engaged on special occasions. The public concert is unknown, and music is a professional art, not a social accomplishment; nevertheless it may be said with truth that for every person in Europe in whose life music is an essential experience, there are, or have been until recently, ten in India. The masters are often the composers of their own songs (poetry and song are inseparable ideas). The words of art songs are short lyrical compositions depicting a single emotional situation and always of high literary merit; but words are used more as a vehicle for the music than for their own sake—words are composed to music rather than music to words. In any case, every performance is in some degree an improvisation; the musician plays or sings in accordance with certain rules and in given modes, but not from a fixed score.

The nearest analogues for the psychic effects of Indian music may be found in plain-song, in troubadour music, mediaeval music generally, and in Bach. The music is devoted to the utterance of a given emotional experience, which is analysed and dwelt upon with overpowering intensity. But, however impassioned, it has none of the *Sturm und Drang* of Beethoven, or the romantic longings of Wagner; it is born of a clear understanding of life. As Fox-Strangways has said, writing from a Western point of view, 'we do not know what to make of music which is dilatory without being sentimental, and utters passion without vehemence'.

**Dictionary of Modern Music and Musicians*, London and Toronto, pp. 248-50.

INDIAN MUSIC

The Indian scale consists of 22 notes (16 only in the southern system), of which 7 correspond to the white notes of the piano, if we imagine the piano tuned in a just and not a tempered scale. The 7 notes are known by the names *Sa, Ri, Ga, Ma, Pa, Dha, Ni,* used in the same way as the syllabic names in the Solfa system. The other notes are sharps or flats of these, and are distinguished by qualifying adjectives. All Indian music is modal, and only a selection of not more than 7 of these notes can be used in any one composition, except as grace-notes. All Indian music is melodic; without actual or implied harmony, other than the tonic note or drone which remains constant in all modes, and is pitched to suit the singer's voice. A characteristic use of grace-notes and sliding progressions produces a colour variation such as is obtained in harmonized music only by varying degrees of assonance.

The fundamental conception in Indian music is that of *rāga,* a word meaning passion or colouring. In the usual classification there are 6 *rāgas,* each with 5 *rāginīs,* the *rāginī* being a modification of the *rāga.* The term is best translated as 'melody-mould'; this melody-mould consists of a selection of 5, 6, or 7 notes distributed over the scale, employing certain characteristic progressions, and laying particular stress on one note, which however, is not to be regarded as a 'key-note'. Every song or composition must conform to and adhere to the peculiarities of the *rāga* or *rāginī* in which it is made. The form of the *rāga* being known, the simple names *Sa, Ri,* etc., suffice for teaching or notation. Notation is little used; singing or playing is never from fixed scores, and every performance is in part an improvisation within the given limits. The *rāgas* are proper to particular seasons and hours, and have definite emotional and ethical associations (*ethos,* as in ancient Greek music). These associations are described in sets of verse called *Rāgamālās,* and illustrated in pictures.

The second essential in Indian music is *tāla* or time-measure. These measures are inseparably connected with the metres of verse (in the East, all poetry is sung or chanted, and never read in a speaking voice); and are therefore based on quantity and not on accent (words are set to music, rather than music to words). Over 100 *tālas* are known, but by no means all are in use. All are combinations of 1, 2, 3, 5, 7, or 9 time-units, each of which may be split up into smaller component parts. The art of the drummer is developed to a point unknown in the West.

Consult: A.H. Fox-Strangways, *Music of Hindustan* (Oxford, 1914); Ratan Devi, *Thirty Indian Songs* (London,1913); E. Clemens, *Introduction to the Study of Indian Music* (London,1913); H.A. Popley, *The Music of India* (Calcutta and London, 1921), and references in article on Indian Musical Instruments.

INDIAN MUSICAL INSTRUMENTS

The voice, in India, is regarded as the chief and noblest of instruments: vocal music therefore has a higher relative valuation than in the West, and is more highly developed.

Next in importance to the voice is the classical *vīṇā,* a kind of lute with 7 long metal strings and 24 frets. Of these strings, 3 are placed on one side and only used to make a drone accompaniment, and to mark time. A common tuning is CGC, and GCG_1 The *vīṇā* is a superb instrument with a vibrant ringing tone, not very loud. Equally with the human voice it is capable of very subtle inflections and graces, inasmuch as whole passages, especially the elaborate trills, shakes and slides which are an essential part of the melodic structure of Indian music and the most obvious vehicle of its peculiar appeal, can be played by a deflection of the long strings, without fresh plucking. In these deflections a range of as much as 4 semitones may be covered, and they lend themselves especially to *pp* effects. A Bengali instrument, similar in principle but deeper in tone, is the *surbahār.*

The *tambura* is a similar instrument without frets, tuned $GCCC_1$. Pieces of silk are placed between the bridge and the strings to produce the buzzing tone, which is like a swarm of bees or the sound of an electric fan. All of the strings are struck by the fingers in rapid succession, so as to produce a continuous drone; this continuous drone is very rich in overtones, and sounds almost like a combination of instruments, never becoming monotonous. The *tambura* is used exclusively as the background of song, with or without the drum.

The instruments played with a bow (*sitār, esraj, sāraṅgī,* etc.) though they have been in use for many centuries, are mainly North Indian, and probably of Persian origin. The *sāraṅgī* is something like a viola in effect; but has from 15 to 20 sympathetic strings, and is mainly used to accompany dancing, together with the drum.

The flute (*venu, muralī*) is one of the most ancient of Indian instruments, and has an important place in literature in connection with the Kṛṣṇa legends, where its sound represents the call to 'leave all and to follow Me'.

Drums are of very many kinds and uses. The drum provides the tonic to which other instruments must be tuned. In certain varieties one or both heads are loaded with special compositions to produce the required tonal effects.

Ensemble consists as a rule of voice, *tambūrā* and drum, or of *vīṇā* and drum. More numerous orchestras in which wind instruments (including the oboe) and drums are conspicuous are used in processional, wedding and martial music. Bands of this type are usually stationed at palace gates, and play all day.

Consult: C.R. Day, *Music and Musical Instruments of Southern India and the Deccan* (London, 1891); C. Sachs, *Die Musikinstr, Indiens und Indonesiens* (Berlin,1914); A.M. Meerwarth, *Guide to the Collection of Musical Instruments in the Indian Museum* (Calcutta, 1917), and references in article on Indian Musical Instruments.

16. Music of East and West*

by Rabindranath Tagore translated by Ananda Coomaraswamy and Kali Mohan Ghose

When I was in Brighton, I went to a concert to hear the songs of a famous singer. I have forgotten her name—probably it was Madame Nilsson or Madame Albani. I had never heard a voice of such wonderful power. In our land even great musicians cannot refrain from attempting to sing any song—even those whose voice cannot easily manage the high or low notes feel no shame in performing indifferently; because in our country, those of the audience who are appreciative, are content to perfect the song in their own mind, by the force of their own feeling. For this reason they regard indifferently the technical perfection of the singing of sweet songs by a singer with a fine voice; because of the external harshness and a certain degree of imperfection the real nature of the thing, finds expression, as it were without any veil. It is like the outward poverty of Maheśvara—in which his glory is nakedly revealed.

In Europe this idea does not exist at all. There the outside finish must be flawless; there it is impossible to appear before an audience, if there are any defects of presentation. We do not at all mind waiting if they sit on the stage for half-an-hour turning the pegs of the *tambūrā* and hammering the *tablas* with the sound of *tak tak;* but in Europe all this preparation is hidden behind the curtain; there, what is done in front, must be quite perfect, and so even the least weakness in a musician's voice is not tolerated.

In our country the first thought is of devotion to the song, and in the songs there are all sorts of difficulties; in Europe, the first object is devotion to the voice, and with the voice, they perform miracles. In our country those who constitute the real audience are content to listen to the song alone; but the European audience listens to the singing of the song. That day in Brighton I found the singer's singing of the songs was wonderfully strange; it seemed to me that she was driving a circus horse in her voice. The movement of the melody passing through her throat nowhere met with the least obstruction. But however much I was astonished that day, I was not touched by the songs. Now and then, in particular, there was an imitation of the singing of birds,

* *The Hindustan Review*, Calcutta, December 1913, pp. 927-9.

which seemed very curious. On the whole, my only impression was that the nature of the human voice was overstepped. Afterwards, listening to the voices of the male singers, I was refreshed—especially by the kind called tenor, for the most part this was *not* like the formless lamentation of a benighted stormy wind, and the lineaments of the human voice were recognizable.

Subsequently by repeated hearing and study of the songs, I acquired some taste for European music. But even now I cannot help feeling that the habitations of European song, and of ours, are, so to speak, quite different; they do not enter the same chamber of the heart, just by the same door. European music, so to speak, is mixed with the actualities of life; we find that we can connect the air of a song with various sorts of events and anecdotes. But if we went on like that with country's singing, it would be ridiculous and uninteresting. Our music, as it were, moves above the incident of daily life, and because of that it is so full of detachment and tenderness—as if it were appointed to reveal the beauty of the innermost and unutterable mystery of the human heart and of the world. That place of mystery is very quiet, solitary, and deep; there is created a forest asylum for the lovers of God, and a bower of delight for the lovers of Beauty, but there is no good provision for the worldling who is wrapped up in activities.

I must not say that I have been unable to enter the heart of European music. But so far as I could grasp it from outside, European singing attracted only one part of my heart. It seems to me that this music is *romantic.* Just what romantic means, it is difficult to explain clearly; but speaking generally the romantic tendencies are those of variety and superfluity, the billows of the ocean of life, the reaction of the conflict of light and shade over restless movement though in another direction there is a broad expanse which has all the stillness of the blue of the sky and is an intimation of the infinite upon the far horizon. The point may not be quite clear; but as I again enjoyed the taste of European music. I said to myself 'It is romantic'. It translates the multifariousness of human life into the sounds of music. It is not that such an attempt is never made in our own music, but that it cannot be vigorous or suggesting that. Our songs speak of the early dawn and the embroidered starry midnight sky of India; our song is the world sundered separation, pain of dripping rain, and the wordless ecstasy of the deep madness of new spring as it reaches the utmost limit of the forests.

By invitation of the Bethune Society I had to read a paper at the Medical College Hall (in Poona) on the eve of my departure for England; it was the first time I read a paper at any meeting. Old Reverend Krishna Mohan Bandhopadhyaya was in the chair, and the subject of the paper was Music. Leaving aside instrumental music, and considering only vocal music, I tried to explain that its main object is by means of the tune to make the words explicit. The written part of my paper was very small; almost from beginning to end I tried to support my thesis by examples by singing the tunes appropriate to different sentiments. I was well rewarded when he said to me 'Hail, Valmiki nightingale'; and the chief cause of that, I think was that I was still very young, and his heart was melted by hearing all those songs sung in a childish treble.

But the opinion I then expressed with so much pride I should now recognize to be false. The art of music has its own nature and special function. Though there are words in a song, *still* they ought not to count for more than the song itself; they are only its vehicle. Song is glorious in its own right; why should it accept the slavery of words? Song begins where words end. The inexpressible is the domain of music. It can say what words cannot; so that the less the words of the song disturb the song, the better. In Hindustani music the words are generally so insignificant that the tune can easily surpass them, and offers its own petition. There, then, is the skill of music, where the *rāginī* as a mere tune mysteriously moves our hearts. But in Bengal the influence of words has been for a long time so strong that pure music has not been able to attain independent power; in this country she must live under the shelter of her sister Poetry. From the rhymed songs of the Vaiṣṇava poets to those of Nidi Babu, subject always, she has tried to utter her charm. But just as in our country a wife can rule her husband by submission to him, so here also music, accepting the duty of obedience to words, has surpassed them.

I have felt this again and again when composing songs. When I began to write a line, humming 'Do not hide in your heart, O Sakhi, your secret words', then I saw that wherever the tune flew away with the words, the words could not follow on foot. Then it seemed to me as if the secret word that I prayed to hear was lost in the gloom of the forest, it melted into the still whiteness of the full moonlight, it was veiled in the blue distance of the horizon—as though it were the innermost secret word of the whole land and sea and sky.

I heard when I was very young the song 'Who dressed you like a foreigner?' and that one line of the song painted such a strange picture in my mind, that even now it is sounding in my memory. I once tried to compose a song myself, under the spell of that line. As I hummed the tune, I wrote the first line of the song—'I know thee, thou Stranger'—and if there were no tune to it, I don't know what meaning would be left in the song. But by the power of the spell (*mantra*) of the tune the mysterious figure of that stranger was evoked in my mind. My heart began to say, 'There is a stranger going to and fro in this world of ours—her house is on the further shore of an ocean of mystery—sometimes she is to be seen in the autumn morning, sometimes in the flowery midnight—sometimes we receive an intimation of her in the depths of our heart—sometimes I hear her voice when I turn my ear to the sky. The tune of my song led me to the very door of that stranger who ensures the universe and appears in it, and I said—

> Wandering over the world,
> I come to thy land;
> I am a guest at thy door, thou Stranger.

One day many days afterwards there was someone going along the road singing—

How does that unknown bird go to and away from the cage?

Could I but catch it, I would put the chain of my mind about its feet! I saw that that Baul song too said the very same thing! Sometimes the unknown bird comes to the closed cage and speaks a word of the limitless Unknown—then the mind would keep it for ever, but cannot. What but the tune of a song could report the coming and going of the unknown bird? Because of this I always feel hesitation in publishing a book of songs, for in such a book the main thing is left out. To set forth the music's vehicle and leave out the music is just like keeping the mouse and leaving out Ganapati himself.

IV. APPENDICES

SECTION A

Mr. Lewis on Indian Music*

The following letter was recently contributed by Dr. Coomaraswamy to the 'Ceylon Observer'.

Dear Sir,

It was with surprise and regret that I read the report of Mr. Lewis' remarks at the Kingswood College prize-giving. I hope he will forgive me for holding up his words to 'execration in the public press'! He said:

> There were some things it was necessary to borrow from the West. Music was one. He had heard that there was such a thing as Eastern music, but he had never been able to appreciate it. That there was something called Eastern music he had good reason to know, for he was treated to it three times a day, or rather twice in the night and once in the day. So far as he could see, Eastern music seemed to have no beginning and no ending, though fortunately it did come to an end.

As a comment upon this I will quote a short extract from a paper I lately wrote on Indian Music for an Indian magazine:

> There is no Indian University where the existence of Indian music or its importance in Indian culture is recognized. Of Europeans engaged in education in India, it is safe to say that less than 1 per cent, if so many, have any knowledge of it as a science, or any appreciation of it as an art. By most it is quite frankly regarded as mere noise and clamour. It is only one illustration of the unfitness of Englishmen to control Indian education; they are unfitted alike by lack of knowledge and by lack of sympathy.

It does not seem to me becoming either, for one who is the successor of kings, who, in the words of the *Mahāvaṁśa*, 'made themselves one with the religion and the people', and who occupies a palace built by them close to the temple in the welfare of which they took so great an interest, should ridicule the daily music there performed. Personally, I like the sound of tom-tomming and the daily *tevava* or musical service of the *vihāras* in Ceylon; but I can quite imagine it possible, and especially for a foreigner, to tire of too much of it. Still, were I in Mr. Lewis' position, I should hardly have liked to say so.

What I equally regret is that he should have gone on, in obvious ignorance, to disparage all Indian, indeed all Eastern, music, very much as if some Eastern visitor in Europe should condemn all European music, having formed his estimate from hearing some provincial street band that disturbed his rest at night. Every suggestion of this kind constantly reiterated from the lips of those in power makes it harder work for those of us who are

** The Ceylon National Review*, Vol. II, No. 5, February 1908, pp. 151-2.

endeavouring to arrest the decay of Indian culture, of which, strange as it may seem to Mr. Lewis, music is a very important part.

Let me explain how the matter can be looked at by ourselves. A Punjabi friend of mine is one of the most cultured men I know—a doctor with German and English qualifications, speaks the four chief European languages fluently, speaks or reads Punjabi, Persian, Hindustani and Sanskrit, beside a little Japanese, has lived in Munich and Vienna and other continental towns, altogether 12 years in Europe, and is married to a Polish lady who is the best amateur pianist known to me, a pupil of Leschetitzky and a friend of Paderewski. In other words, he has had more opportunity of appreciating the beauties of European and the faults of Indian music than most Indians. Yet my friend is today passionately devoted to Indian music; and European music is to him *absolutely meaningless.* In this he does not stand alone amongst cultured Indians; and such cases show how unfair and prejudiced is the ordinary European attitude. There is no more reason for a sweeping condemnation of Indian, than there is for a sweeping condemnation of European, music. Personally, if I had to choose for ever between all European and all Indian music, I should without hesitation choose the Indian; so would my Punjabi friend; so would my wife—an L.R.A.M. of London; but not so would Mr. Lewis. What does it mean? Surely that contemptuous disparagement from either side is out of place, and most of all as from ruler to ruled, for courtesy is especially to be looked for from those in power, in their relations toward those whom they rule.

The Editor "The Observer" Yours faithfully,
Campden, 7 January 1908 A.K. COOMARASWAMY

A Concert of Indian Music*

RATAN DEVI SINGS CLASSICAL RAGAS AND KASHMIRI FOLK SONGS

An exposition of the music of India was given yesterday afternoon. In the Princess Theatre by Ratan Devi, an Englishwoman who has made a deep study of the music under Indian masters, and her husband, Dr. Ananda Coomaraswamy, who is himself a native of India.

Dr. Coomaraswamy first spoke, giving a brief account of the music of India. He told of its great age and of the fact that it is not a popular art relying on the support of the public, but is either maintained under the protection of the aristocracy or is temple music. The Hindu scale differs from the European tempered scale in the use of smaller intervals, of which there are twenty-two to an octave. A *rāga* is a selection of five, six, or seven notes, a more particularized mode; or definite progression, corresponding in some degree with the old ecclesiastical modes of European music. Dr. Coomaraswamy called it a 'ground plan' of a song, on which the singer improvises. The words are regarded as of little consequence and as only a means of embodying the music. Each *rāga* is associated with definite effects, and *rāgas* are 'magical songs' intended to arouse a definite emotion. Singing is thus not an entertainment but a magical ceremony, and the singer's art is not one of self-expression, but the means through which a god or goddess influences humanity.

Ratan Devi appeared in Oriental costume: she sat on the floor between two vases of poinsettias and two pots of burning incense. She held upright the accompanying instrument, the *tambūrā*, and with her right hand played its metallic strings , which have a faint, silvery sound, and are heard in one short melodic figure constantly repeated. With her left hand she made incessant slight gestures. She began with classical Indian *rāgas*. Her voice is a mezzo of agreeable quality, admirably under her control for the production of the effects desired. These, in the *rāgas*, had the effect of improvisation, musically often strangely expressive, not unmelodious in the Occidental sense, adorned occasionally with little flowery passages, and only occasionally showing the unaccustomed intervals peculiar to the Indian scale. They have a strange and weird effect, often a haunting beauty and potency of expression, even to ears unaccustomed.

A group of Kashmiri folk songs was then sung, which Dr. Coomaraswamy explained were true folk songs with the chief importance put upon the words. Ratan Devi appeared in a different costume and sang them without

*Published in some local daily newspaper of USA.

accompaniment. Among them was a group of lullabies. They showed, of course, a marked difference in rhythmic and melodic character from the classic songs and are based on a less complicated scale. Many of these were vivacious, crisply expressive, rhythmically varied.

The exposition of this unfamiliar and exotic art was of great fascination. The singer is an artist who has evidently fully absorbed the Hindu spirit and traditions, as well as the different techniques of the music. Her performance yesterday was heard by a numerous audience with great interest and pleasure; with something quite beyond curiosity.

Indian Music as a Development of Pure Melody*

EDINBURGH, Scotland—Dr. Ananda K. Coomaraswamy, D.Sc., before his return to India via America was presented with an address in the name of the Indian students, of whom there are many resident in Scotland, expressing profound appreciation and gratitude for the eminent services Dr. and Mrs. Coomaraswamy had rendered to India by representing to the European world the true interpretation of their ideas and life, thus giving a fresh impetus to the endeavour to establish a more sympathetic understanding and collaboration between the West and the East.

On this occasion Dr. Coomaraswamy gave a lecture on Indian music, which was illustrated by a recital of Indian music by Mrs. Coomaraswamy. Music in India, the lecturer said, was a professional art cultivated under patronage to a high degree of perfection during the last 2000 years. It represented a development of pure melody and as such was clearly distinguished from the harmonized music of the Western professional school. Every song might be regarded as an improvisation upon a given theme, these themes being known as *rāgas*, or *rāginīs*, a word best translated as melody-mould, that is, something more particularized than an air. Each *rāga* consisted of a scale of five, six or seven notes from a possible scale of 22. As with each *rāga* was associated a definite ethos or sentiment, there was no modulation, hence this would involve a change of motive which it was intended to elaborate. While Western keyed instruments were tempered to facilitate orchestration and change of key, this sacrifice, he said, made for the sake of harmony, had never been made in Indian music, and they had, therefore, they felt, retained the full liberty which belonged to an art based on pure intonation.

*This is a lecture given to the Indian Students at Edinburgh wherein A.K.C. tells of Indian Music as a development of pure melody. It was a Farewell Speech and was given on 11 March 1916. It was later referred to in *The Christian Science Monitor*, Boston, March 1916.

SECTION B

Indian Music as Ananda Coomaraswamy Saw it*

by K.C. Kamaliah

Ananda Coomaraswamy's credentials as a scholar were recognized even while he was in his 30s. His scientific papers no doubt reveal his devotion to science, despite his later gravitation to artistic and philosophic studies. It is neither wise nor prudent to see a split personality in Ananda Coomaraswamy, as though a narrow nationalist changed his colour and bloomed into a broad universalist. One of his early booklets, 'Essays in National Idealism' was brought out when he was only 32. In his own words, 'these essays represent an endeavour towards an explanation of the true significance of the national movement in India'.

Ananda Coomaraswamy significantly observes that 'the two sides of the national movement, the material and the spiritual, are inseparable and must attain success or fail together'. He quotes Confucius: 'When the prince loves what the people love and hates what the people hate, then is he what is called the father of the people'. He adds: 'These ideals are absolutely unattainable by Englishmen in India.'

CLARITY OF THOUGHT

No clash of ideas nor deviation from the accepted moral codes common for mankind can be seen in the utterances of Coomaraswamy. His nationalism is not an antithesis of universalism, but a real synthesis, a union of hearts between the two.

There are three essays pertaining to Indian Music in the collection relating to *National Idealism* and one included in the *Dance of Siva.* These four essays on Indian Music from the pen of Ananda Coomaraswamy would form a priceless treasure in the archives of a musician and a musicologist. Ananda Coomaraswamy's clarity of thought and lucidity have few parallels amongst authors writing on serious topics. 'Music has been a cultivated art in India for at least three thousand years. The chant is an essential element of Vedic ritual; and the references in later Vedic literature, the scriptures of Buddhism and the Brahmanical epics show that it was already highly developed as a secular art in centuries preceding the beginning of the Christian era,' writes Coomaraswamy (*Indian Music* in the *Dance of Siva*).

**Swarajya*, Vol: XXIII, No. 15, Madras, October 1978.

PATRONAGE HAS LAPSED

Music has thrived in India under cultivated patronage. But that was so till at least the forties. With the dawn of independence and the abolition of the princely order preceded by the elimination of the zamidary system, there has been a marked change and cultivated patronage ebbed out of existence. Rural audiences which for centuries were treated to classical music in temples and courts find themselves relegated as non-entities and urban centres are the beneficiaries today. Ananda Coomaraswamy has a word of praise when he says:

> Music has always been the delight of Hindu kings. At their courts were to be found the best musicians. Whatever the luxury or corruption of some Indian courts may at times have been, they were always centres of culture. The place of the royal craftsmen, pandits, astronomers, and musicians were assured; their maintenance belonged to the ideal of kingly state. Culture was thus state-endowed and pursued its way undisturbed by political events.

NO SUBSTITUTE FOR HUMAN VOICE

Ananda Coomaraswamy was greatly moved by the tenderness of Indian music and those who once fall beneath its sway are for ever spellbound by its magic.

> The delicacy and subjectivity of Indian Music cannot move those accustomed to the noisy music of an orchestra, the artificial atmosphere of an upholstered and crowded concert hall. The impression conveyed by Indian music is that of a limpid purity of colour effect, and compared with Western concerted music suggests a comparison of refined and delicate Indian dyes with the brilliant variety of modern chemical colouring matters, or the flow of a deep river with the rush of a noisy torrent,

writes Coomaraswamy. The human voice in music is assigned a high place by the great savant. 'The most perfect music is that of the human voice' are the pregnant words of Coomaraswamy. Even the most perfect machine cannot take the place of a living singer or player.

'The performance of a musician is never exactly repeated on each occasion; he adapts himself insensibly to the different conditions and finds also in himself new expression through the old form. There is moreover his personal influence, the power of his personality, the vision of a living man giving expression to emotions in a disciplined traditional art language'. (*Gramaphones—And Why Not* in *Essays in National Idealism*). The veracity of this observation of Coomaraswamy can be felt taking into account the great singers of Indian music of today and the past. Not without reason Tiruvalluvar assigned a higher place to the human voice than to instrumental music.

> 'The flute is sweet, the lute is sweet, they say
> Who do not hear the merry prattle of their children'. (Tirukkural, 66)

Adiyarkkunallar too, the learned commentator of the *Śilappadhikāram*, while defining the very word, *isai*, links it with human voice. *Isai* derives its name from the many *iyarpas,* conjoined with *niram.* Because of its conjointment—*isaittal,* with literary compositions, the term *isai* came into vogue. Only vocal music was indicated by the term *isai,* in the beginning. Later it came to be applied to music as a whole, vocal or instrumental. Karaikkal Ammaiyar, the saint and musical luminary, connects music with song—*kollentrisaipada.*

INDIAN MUSIC SINCE AGES

As in the case with many arts, early Indian music must have differed much from the modern practice of it. Though the modern theory, modes and notation are derived from the ancients, the differences between them are marked and perceivable.

Coomaraswamy traces even the origin of most of the musical instruments of Europe and says that

> the prototypes of most or all European instruments in use at the present day are still to be found in the East, the source of the foundations of so much western culture. The Greeks attributed the greater part of their science of music to India. Notwithstanding the differences between modern and ancient Hindu music, it is probable that the music of Southern India is more akin to ancient Greek music than any other music remaining in the world. (*Essays in National Idealism*).

What are called Hindustani Music and Carnatic Music have not been dealt with by Coomaraswamy. But perhaps he mentions the latter by the term 'South Indian Music'. 'The form of the Vedic chants is fixed and constant throughout India, but this is not the case with other hymns such as those of the Southern Śaivites, which are sung to many airs in the homes and temples of the South,' writes Coomaraswamy. Apart from the seeming or apparent or real contrast between Hindustani and Carnatic Music systems the *pans* employed in the singing of the Śaivite/Vaiṣṇavite hymns and the mode adopted in the singing of *Tiruppukal* songs must not be forgotten. Though these have a close affinity with Carnatic Music, their separate identity cannot fail to be taken note of.

MOTHER OF INSTRUMENTS

Ananda Coomaraswamy was greatly attracted to the *vīṇā.* No wonder, Tirunavukkarasar called it the flawless *vinai—macil vinai.* 'The *Vīṇā* takes many years to learn. It is easier to pick out notes on harmonium than to play the *vīṇā* or the violin; easier to subscribe for shares in a Swadeshi factory than to re-organize and support a village industry; easier to drift than to swim. But for India is it worthwhile, is this the art of living? Is not an India thus subdued in soul more lost than any India governed by the sword could be?' writes Coomaraswamy. This was how the tormented soul in Coomaraswamy felt about the deterioration in standards in the realm of music. The *vīṇā* kindles in us nostalgic memories of our ancient past. Does it not adorn the hands of the Goddess of Learning? In Tamil literature, it is the *Yal,* a form of lute such as the *vīṇā*, that is famous. *Yal* was perhaps a complicated instrument. *Vīṇā* and *Yal* were tender instruments, deserving a feminine touch. In the *Śilappadhikāram* one reads how the *Yal* is being handled by Matavi before being handed over to Kovalan.

> Matavi made her obeisance to the *Yal* while receiving it on the seashore in Pukar. The *Yal* looked a handsome bride with dark eyes made darker with collyrium, free from the faults of *pattar, kodu, ani* and strings. In order to test its worthiness, she tuned it (*pannal*), caressed the strings with her fingers (*parivattam*), checked the pitch of each note (*araytal*), just touching the strings (*taivaral*), exhibited rhythm, melody and the like and passed on (*celavu*), blending the vocal songs to the rhythmic beats from the strings (*vilaiyattu*), made herself one with pleasure (*kaiyul*) and adjusted herself to the instrument (*kurumpokku*). Her tender fingers emitting lustre from the many gems on them traversed the strings as bees on a flower and as laid down by musical experts; she further tested the instrument by plucking (*vartal*), caressing (*vadittal*), pushing forward (*untal*), rubbing (*teruttal*) and (*pattadai*), one of the movements in playing a lute. (*Śilappadhikāram, Kanalvari*)

What has been quoted above equally applies to the *vīṇā*.

Ananda Coomaraswamy gives a pride of place to the *vīṇā*. His considered views are:

> India has, besides the *tambūrā*, many solo instruments. By far the most important of these is the *vīṇā*. This classic instrument, which ranks with the violin of Europe and the kota of Japan and second only to the voice in sensitive response, differs chiefly from the *tambūrā* in having frets, the notes being made with the left hand and the strings plucked with the right. The delicate nuances of micro-tonal grace are obtained by the deflection of the strings, whole passages being played in this manner solely by a lateral movement, without a fresh plucking. While the only difficulty in playing the *tambūrā* is to maintain an even rhythm independently of the songs, the *vīṇā* presents all the difficulties of technique that can be imagined, and it is said that at least twelve years are required to attain proficiency.

The *vīṇā* has been a prestigious musical instrument in Tamilnadu and one can remember names belonging to the fair sex, noted for their mastery over the playing on the *vīṇā*. Though there are *vīṇā* maestros among men too, it is an instrument better suited to and played by the fair sex. It may be conceded that the *vīṇā* is not a musical instrument exclusively handled by women.

VĪṆĀDHARA DAKṢIṆĀMŪRTI

One comes across a Vīṇādhara Dakṣiṇāmūrti in sculptures. Ananda Coomaraswamy describes a copper image kept in the Museum of Fine Arts, Boston: 'Śiva (Vīṇādhara Dakṣiṇāmūrti) as teacher of music. Three eyed, four armed, standing figure the *sama* or *abhaṅga* pose the l.r. and the l.l arms held as if playing the *vīṇā*, the u.r.h. in *kartarī mukha* pose holding the axe (*paraśu* or *ṭaṅka*) the l.r.h. in the same pose holding the black (*mṛga*).' Śiva as teacher of the *śāstras* (scripture), of *jñāna* (illumination), of *yoga* (union) and of *saṅgīta* (music) is known as Dakṣiṇāmūrti: there being four types of images, according to the subject of instruction. The Dakṣiṇāmūrti aspect of Śiva is always invoked by students of the sciences and arts.

In his very famous *Tevaram* song Sambandhar refers to the playing on the *vīṇā* by Śiva, which denotes His act of destruction, one of the five acts of God—*veyuru toli pankan vidamunda kantan mika nalla vinai tadavi.* Thirunavukkarasar depicts in one of his *Tevaram* hymns the Lord playing on the *vīṇā*, when the universe perishes:

With deluge overtaking and
submerging vast oceans
Brahmā enveloped in a watery
grave and unrest reigning,
Added to it He of the hue of
blue sea perishing in confusion,
Waters retreating, My Lord as
Kaṅkāla plays on the vīṇā superb.

Śiva as Kaṅkālamūrti is a very popular theme with the Nayanmars. Manikkavasakar refers to the same. There are some beautiful bronzes of Kaṅkālamūrti in the temples of the Tamil Country. Kaṅkālamūrti as sculptured resembles Bhikṣāṭanamūrti, with the difference, that the Lord is not nude and carries on His shoulders a bundle of bones of many Brahmās and Viṣṇus dangling from the stick thrown across His shoulder.

UNDERSTANDING OURSELVES

Ananda Coomaraswamy is very clear that a pretence at the same time of despising Indian and of admiring European music is ridiculous for a true Indian. 'Western culture may be, and will be of value to the East, but it must be as a post-graduate course—it will not stand in the place of mother milk. We cannot understand others by ceasing to understand ourselves.' Coomaraswamy was a knowledgeable person. He was dead against the harmonium and the gramaphone. 'In the first place, to a person of culture—especially musical culture—the sound of a gramophone is not an entertainment, but the refinement of torture.' When compared to stringed instruments, even the piano, according to Coomaraswamy, is relatively an inferior instrument.

It is a bit difficult to imagine how Ananda Coomaraswamy would have reacted to listening to songs set to music following the western pattern. Ananda Coomaraswamy warns:

> One cannot gather grapes of thorns. You cannot in the long run get something for nothing. Do not let us pretend that it is possible. If our ideal is one of purely material prosperity, and we have no time for music or the arts, let us have done with them altogether. But if we think of the most real part of our lives let us cherish them accordingly. (*Music and Education in India* in the *Essays In National Idealism*)

The prophetic words of Ananda Coomaraswamy are valid even today.

Music in Ceylon*

The following represent an attempt to write down in English notation, some Tamil tunes as they were heard sung in Jaffna sometime ago. They were written down as representing, as nearly as possible, in English notation the actual notes that were sung, without then knowing much of the intricacies of Tamil music. No. 1, 'Kadaiyevane' was sung to some verses from the Tiruvacagam, by two different singers. No. 2 is the same tune but sung to different words, also out of the Tiruvacagam. (This one and the next were given to me by Mrs. Tiru-Navuk-Arasu). Nos. 3 and 4 are Tevaram.

This attempt at writing down in English notation, a few Tamil tunes, has made me realize how impossible it is to at all adequately represent Tamil

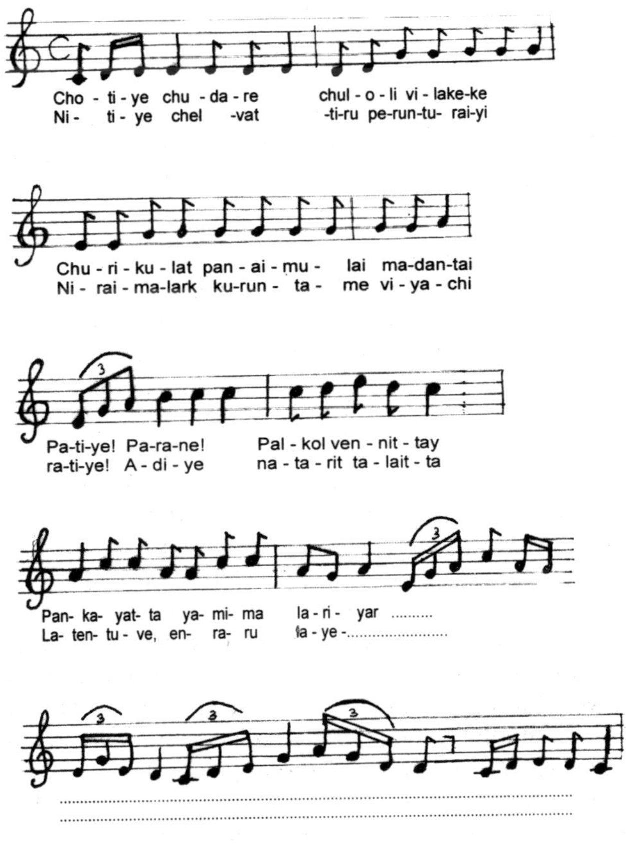

The 'Decade of Grace' or 'cleansing from Delusion' Tiruvacagam

*S. Durai Raja Singam, *A Personal Approach*, Vol. I, pp. 189-91.

music by Western methods, and that if much of this is done, the inevitable result will be the decline of Indian music. The modern tendency in Indian music is to more and more eliminate the delicate shades of intervals of which it is so full, and to limit it more to the whole tone and half tone intervals. If some method could be arrived at to indicate 1/3 and 1/4 tones, then the attempt might be followed with better success: this would be by no means impossible, and it would then exclude the use of the piano and such like instruments from attempting the impossible. One or more of the airs here given however are written in modes which do not include 1/4 or 1/3 tones, and thus better adapted for recording in staff notation.

Vidalalavayilay

Indian music can only be represented either by the voice or by stringed instruments. To attempt to play the notes on a piano must result in a miserable fiasco. The piano developed with modern harmony; where melody alone is concerned, it is useless. The harmonic combinations to which the Western ear is accustomed, is in Indian music compensated for by greater freedom in melodic intervals: the elaborate use of harmony, such as has been reached in the West, is quite impossible to combine with the melodic system of the East, and also is felt to be unnecessary. To quite realize this, one must hear first the mere melody of an English tune sung or played, and then an Indian air. In the English air a harmony is indeed needed its baldness is too apparent; but in the other the shades and developments of the melody alone are quite sufficient to satisfy the ear. Perhaps what strikes a foreign ear in first listening to Indian music is the softness and sweetness of the music as compared with the noisy tangle of sound in Western music. One realizes then only, the true and infinite value of pure melody. It is like turning from the roaring rocky stream to the quiet flowing river. I do not mean thus to depreciate Western music, because it also has its glories, but I do mean to say that a Western who knows nothing of Indian music, has missed something that he can ill afford to miss. The music of the Greeks was probably near akin to it; and ancient European plainsong has something of the same effect. But it is not possible at all to compare it with modern harmonized music; music

Kunttin

in the West and in the East have trodden different paths, one has developed harmony, the other melody. To attempt a combination of the two is as foolish and unscientific as it is impossible. For the revival of the study of Indian music in Ceylon, two principal things are necessary; the cultivation of the voice, and that I believe only the West can teach the East; and the study of Indian instruments.

For the Revival of the study of Indian music in Ceylon, two principal things are necessary; the cultivation of the voice, and that I believe only the West can teach the East; and the study of Indian instruments.

ETHEL COOMARASWAMY*

*The first wife of A.K. Coomaraswamy.

Thevaram According to Pann*

When Coomaraswamy visited the Jaffna Hindu College on June 4, 1906 he gave five thousand rupees for teaching and training the students to sing *Thevarams* according to *Pan*[1] (harmonious sound or musical mode or tune). Coomaraswamy insisted that *Thevarams* should be sung strictly according to traditions and in their original *panns* without setting them to new tunes.[2] The hymns of the three Śaivaite saints Tirugnana Sambandar, Thirunavukarasu, and Sundara Murti Nayanar and the *Thiruvacakam* of Mannikavasagar form the bulk of verses in the *Peniniruthirumurai.* The deity that forms the main theme of these devotional hymns which formed the bulk of Tamil literature in the seventh century. The Śaivaite saints were those responsible for this change in the field of literature.

The Śaivaite faith was thus propagated through these devotional hymns. *Pann*[3] in the music of the Tamils was what *rāgas* were in Sanskrit texts. The *Oduvars* take the pride of place in temple rituals and Thevaram music. All these saints visualized Śiva as *Naṭarāja.* They called him *Manradi* (the Dancer at the audience-hall); *Pennarupagan* when he shared half his body with Devī; Chudalai Adir or *Chudalai Pemmar* (when he wielded his power at cremation ground).

The population of north Ceylon (Jaffna) is predominantly Tamil and the religion of the people is Śaivaism, to a very large extent. The propagation of Śaivaism in Jaffna was by the first Singai-Aryan. The King in a dream saw Śiva (with Pārvatī) declaring himself to be Kayilaya Nathan. He was requested by Śiva to build a temple, the Kailāsanātha Koil at Nallur. Nallur was known as another Kayilayam, the first being at Mount Kailāsa, the second at Chidambaram, and the third at Koneśvaram.

The Hindu revival in Jaffna, after the Portuguese and Dutch rule and during the British period was brought about by Sri La Sri Arumuga Navalar, 'the Champion Reformer of the Hindus' in the tradition of the Indian saints. He was the father of both Hindu education and Tamil prose in the country. For full details see (a) Kailasapillay, T. *Arumuganavalar Charithiram*; Vidyanubbhana Press, Madras, Third Edition, 1950; (b) *Sri La Sri Arumuga Navalar, A Biographical Study*, Saiva Prakasa Press, Jaffna, 1965.

* S. Durai Raja Singam, *A Personal Approach*, Vol. II, pp. 153-4.

NOTES

1. The Award has now been revived by the author.
2. There are Pann Research Societies and Organizations today. The Academy of Tamil Music in Madras has been carrying out commendable research work on pans in *Thevaram*. The researchers have brought to light a few facts. For instance, let us take *yal murip pann*. A song by the saint Sambandar begins with these words, *Madar madappidi*. This is being sung now in the Atana *rāga*. The researchers show that only fifty years ago one Guruswamy Desikar started to sing this song in Atana; and others have taken it up since then; but before the period of Guruswamy Desikar it was sung in Megarāga krucini. Many pieces of information like this can come to light through the research of the Academy. A *pan* is a primary melody type; the *rāga* in Carnatic, and *rāg* in Hindustani music.
3. The word *Pann* meaning music, which dominates any study of Tamil Music, finds a place in this ancient work. A number of other words related to *Pann*, such as *Pannai*—the place where music is sung, and *Pannathi*—a poem set to music are also to be found. We are also told that there were several kinds of artists, who constituted essential elements of ancient society. They were the *kuthar* (dancer and dramatist), *panar* and *porunar*, the musician, and *virali*, the lady artist. The *panars* themselves were further subdivided into *peria-panar* and *siria-panar*, possibly based on the size and scope of the instruments played on by them.—V.P. Raman in 'The Music of the Ancient Tamils', paper read in Kuala Lumpur, 1956.

*Thevaram**

Among the Śaiva community in South India and Jaffna, the Śaivite saints, Sambandar, Apparswami, Sundaramurti, Manikkavachakar and Tayumanavar are held in great veneration. There is scarcely a Śaiva temple in these places where their images are not daily worshipped. In most of these temples and Hindu assembly halls special annual functions and *pūjās* are held to invoke their spiritual aid. Their hymns and songs were arranged into eleven groups or *Tirumurai* by a Brahmin priest Nambi Andar Nambi. The first three contain those of Sambandar, the next three Appar (also called Tirunavukarasu). The seventh comprises the hymns of Sundaramūrti. These seven collections form the compilation called *Devaram* or *Thevaram.* They are sung on ceremonial or religious occasions. Learning by heart of them is held to be a virtue. Public recitation after the *pūjās* in temples are held. These are sung according to *pann.* Coomaraswamy, was a firm believer in the efficacy of *thevarams* sung according to *pann.*

The twelve Tirumurais cover a period of six centuries for the seventh to the twelfth century AD. Nambi-andar-nambi, a Brahmin of Navriyur, near Chidambaram compiled the *Thevaram* hymns and classified them. He classified the twelve Śaivite *Tirumurais* but only the compilation of the first seven is attributed to him. Appar and Sundarar lived in the middle of the seventh century and Sundarar probably in the ninth century. The Chola kings patronized the recital of hymnal literature.

Like Tiruvalluvar and Manimekalai the three saints emphasized the virtue of hospitality and the giving of alms. Offering of boiled rice to the crows is one of the religious customs. *Pali* is the word mentioned in the hymns which means crow (used in the hymns as food given to Lord Śiva).

The three saints always associated art with God. There are numerous references in their hymns to Painting, Architecture, Music and Dance.

They were great exponents of the Śaiva Siddhānta philosophy. Like Saint Manikkavachakar they were for tolerance in attitudes towards other religions and oneness of God. This view has been corroborated in *Civananaattiyar,* a work in Śaiva Siddhānta philosophy. Coomaraswamy has in his writings maintained that all paths lead to the same summit.

The music of the *thevaram* (offering to God) is perhaps the oldest form of temple music apart from Vedic chant. They are performed daily by hereditary *thevaram* families in the precincts of temples. The *rāga* in old Tamil is *pann.*

Coomaraswamy has written several articles on Indian music with references to the *vīṇā.* Some of these are listed below:

* S. Durai Raja Singam, *A Personal Approach,* Vol. III, p. 173.

1924 'Music in India, Indian Music, Indian Musical Instruments,' in *Dictionary of Modern Music and Musicians*, London and Toronto.

1930 'The Parts of a Vina,' *Journal of the American Oriental Society*, New Haven, Connecticut, Vol. L, pp. 244-53. There is one plate of six figures, depicting the old Indian *vīṇā* in use besides two other figures, one of the old Indian *harp-vīṇā* and the other of the old Indian *vīnā* or mandolin. The various parts of the *vīṇā* are then described with a list of illustrations on the plate.

1931 'The Old Indian Vina', *Journal of the American Oriental Society*, New Haven, Connecticut, Vol LI, pp. 47-50, 1 plate.

There is one figure included, which depicts a Dancing scene showing the lute and the harp-*vīṇā*. It is from an architrave at Pawaya, Gwalior. The reproduction of the Pawaya dancing scene shows both the lute and the harp-*vīṇā* very clearly. The article discusses Canon Gilpins 'learned discussion of Sumerian harps in *Music and Letters*, for April, 1929'. The presence of bow-shaped harps in India is pointed out by A.K.C. Details of the harp in Java and Burma are also mentioned.

1931 'Upavina', *Journal of the American Oriental Society*, New Haven, Connecticut, Vol. LI, pp. 284-5.

Coomaraswamy writes: In my discussion of the *Parts of a vīṇā* (*JAOS*, 50.244-53, see especially p. 252) the meaning of this term was not clearly ascertained. Mr. P.V. Bapat now points out to me that in the *Visuddhimagga*, Ch. 20 (PTS, ed., p. 630) the sound is said to be produced because of the *vīṇā, upavīna,* and a man's suitable effort. Dhammapāla in his Commentary explains *upavīna* as *vīṇā-vidāna.* Ganthi, a later commentator, explains it as something made of ivory or horn, requisite to the *upadhamsana* has meaning such as 'urging, inciting, producing', and must here refer to the production of sound by striking. It would therefore seem very evident that *upavīna*, literally '*vīṇā*-accessory' must = 'plectrum'. However, if this be so, it is not clear why *upavīna* and *koṇa* should be mentioned together in the Miln. 53, and SN IV.197 lists. In the latter, the Comm. has *upavena* = *upadharana* = *vethaka*, which should mean some kind of wrapping; cf. *patia.* It is stated that the sound is produced by the *koṇa*, i.e. the plectrum, combined with the proper effort of the player (*kona* is glossed *cuturansa-saldandaka*, 'a four-cornered piece of *sana*-wood'); this compared with the *Visudhimagga* passage again suggests that *upavīna* = *koṇa.* Against this is the list of parts, mentioning both. In any case *upavīna* is not 'bridge' as the PTS translation has it. The following are additional references to parts of a *vīṇā*: *Visuddhimagga*, 251, *vinadonikonaddhacamma*, 'skin stretched over the belly of the *vīṇā*'; ib., 354, the *mahāvīṇā* is covered with wet ox-hide; ib., 594, *doni, tanti.*

1934 '*Die Vina und der Indische Tonsystem bei Bharata*, Zeitscrift fur vergleichende Musikivissenchraft', Vol. III, p. 83.

1935 'A Passage on Vina Playing', *Seitschr fur vergleischende Musikwissenschaft*, III, p. 88.

1937 'The Parts of a Vina', *Journal of the American Oriental Society*, New Haven, Connecticut, Vol. LVII, pp. 101-3.

Coomaraswamy continues his discussion on the terminology of the parts of the old Indian pastless harp by giving an English rendering with brief comment. The previous artiles were published in *JAOS* 50.244. and 51.47 and 284.

It was my good fortune to have been Swami Vipulanands's (earlier konwn as Pandit Mylvaganam) pupil at Manipay Hindu College. When I met him last in 1946, at the Ramakrishna Mission, Wellaiwalten he told me that it was the writings of Coomaraswamy on the *vīṇā* that led him to begin his work on the *Yal Nool*—this fact he has respectfully mentioned in his monumental which was released in 1947. Soon after its publication he passed away in July 1947.

Swami Vipulananda mentions in his *Yal Nool* that 'The sculpture at Amaravati belonging to the period of *Śilapadikaram* depicts a *yal* with more than seven strings. Ananda Coomaraswamy, a scholar from Jaffna and a great authority on art was shown a photocopy of this sculpture. Coomaraswamy explained that this antique musical instrument was used in Tamil Nadu during the period of *Śilapadikaram* and that an ancient music tradition existed in Tamil Nadu which is now extinct.' The Swamiji further mentioned that 'the difference between *vīṇā* and *Yal* is explained in great detail in "The Legacy of India" edited by G.T. Garrat (Oxford University Press). The *Yal* which was originally used by the folk singers, both male and female, was later used by dancers and musicians during the time of Ilanko Atikal. As was customary then, the *yal* was decorated "like a bride with folwers". During the lifetime of Aludaiya Pilla (*St. Sambandar*) the *Yal* was used to spread the Bakti cult by means of devotional music. In the epic poems of Tirutakka Tevar and Kongu Velir. The *Yal* was instrumental to unite lovers. The *Yal* which is totally extinct today, had grown out of the *viliyal*, *ciriyal* and *periyal*, and during its development it was greatly cherished and patronised by singers, musicologists, kings and devotees. Along with the *yal*, the tradition of reciting *pan* has also disappeared. When Tirumuraikanta colan (Raja Raja I) brought to light the hidden hymns pf *Tevaram* and developed the art of singing *Pan*, he was assisted by a lady who was a descendant of Tirunilakante yalpanar. There are no documents relating to the theory of the branch of music. However, a fragmentary information is available from the book "Saṅgitha Ratnākara" of Śāraṅgadeva of the 13th century in which the music of certain hymns of Tevaram is explained.' (The quotation is based on extracts from the *Yal Nool*, which is in Tamil.)

The artist had to play on the *yal* by skilfully combining the seven notes of the diatonic scale (*elicai*); and *Yal venri* refers to the triumph of the artist over his musical instrument. In ancient Tamil Nadu, *Yal* was very popular. It is no longer in use now; the *vīṇā* has suplanted it.

A stanza, beginning with *palai padumalai* in a literary work called *Perumtinai* has a description of a woman artist's virtuoso performance. Here is a paraphrase of the stanza*: She took the *yal* in her hands. It was of the small kind, and beautifully made. She played the seven melodies of *palaip pan* so divinely that her listeners became spell bound.

This musical instrument known as *yal* was widely played throughout India in the past. Even after it went out of vogue in North India, it was popular in Tamil Nadu for a long time/until the eleventh century AD, and then it disappeared from the scene. The *pans* connected with the *yal* are quite ancient. The *pans* that were played in the times of Sambandar, Sundarar, Thiruppanalvar, Thiruneelakanda Yalppanar, Panappattirar, etc., and in the Sangam period which predates them, were related to the music of *Yal.*

Swami Vipulananda, the great Tamil scholar has recreated the *Yal* after a great deal of research and study. Unfortunately he died before pulling the instrument into use.

*Based on the commentary by Makaralur Kilan Camundevan.

Index